C★L★A★S★S★I★C
AMERICAN NATURAL DESSERTS
COOKBOOK

DAVID SMITHER

AVERY PUBLISHING GROUP INC.
Garden City Park, New York

Cover Design: Ann Vestal
Front Cover Photograph Credit: John Harper
Front Cover Food Stylist: Dianne Harper
Back Cover Photograph: "Fireworks" by Howard Earl Simmons
In-House Editor: Linda Comac
Typesetter: Bonnie Freid

*TX
773
.S63
1993*

Library of Congress Cataloging-in-Publication Data

Smither, David.
   Classic American Natural Desserts Cookbook / David Smither.
      p.   cm.
   Includes bibliographical references and index.
   ISBN 0-89529-527-X : $9.95
      1. Desserts—United States. 2. Cookery, American. 3. Cookery
(Natural foods)   I. Title.
TX773.S63   1993   92-35089
641.8'6—dc20   CIP

Printed in the United States of America.

10 9 8 7 6 5 4 3 2 1

Contents

Preface . . . . *vii*

Introduction 1

Cakes 5

Cookies 43

Pies and Pastries 63

Puddings 105

Candies, Frostings, Glazes 123

Cooling Desserts 145

Beverages 171

Bibliography 185

Index 187

To my wife, Anita,
and my son, Jonathan,
for their love and "feed" back.

Preface

Several years ago, I set out on a somewhat desperate quest for a dessert cookbook in which the recipes called for natural ingredients including sweeteners such as honey, molasses, and pure maple syrup. My family and I had sworn off processed sugars and flours, preservatives, and dyes. Almost immediately, we began to reap the tremendous benefits of a healthier life style. Miraculously, allergies and asthma disappeared, and along with them, weekly shots and mounting medical bills. We became "radical converts" and were eyed with suspicion by relatives and friends. Although they admired our determination and self-discipline, they did not share our enthusiasm for our culinary offerings . . . especially desserts. Those first holiday dinners with relatives and church friends were most revealing. Their comment was, "You bring the green salad; we'll bring the dessert." The message was clearer yet when our son's teen-age friends volunteered to bring their own "goodies" for overnight gatherings.

It was obvious that the recipes and cookbooks I had amassed, though attractive and practical in other ways, did not produce desserts that were sweet enough for those accustomed to refined sugars. I had no alternative but to produce my own collection of natural dessert recipes.

It was not, however, my original purpose to actually write a book for others to use and enjoy. I would have been content to have scribbled a few lines on index cards for quick reference. After all, cooking is just a hobby. By profession, I am a composer-musician and the author of eight books on keyboard music. And like many people involved in a demanding profession, I get pleasure and just the right amount of diversion by creating a new recipe to please my family. I love the challenge of occasionally producing an original recipe that is not simply an adaptation of one using processed sweeteners and refined flours. But my audience would not let me be satisfied with so little. My family encouraged and cajoled; they made suggestions for other things I could make. Our local health-food-store owners—amazed that my desserts were as sweet as those using processed sweeteners—suggested that there was a market for my recipes and that I should write a book.

With God's helpful inspiration, and encouragement from my wife and son, the collection did grow into a book. As I wrote, I determined to create classic dessert recipes that would "fool" even the most ardent sugar lover. I would be satisfied only when "unconverted" friends and relatives asked for second helpings. When two of my original candy recipes took ribbons at the Panhandle South Plains Fair, I knew the "quest" was ended. I had written the cookbook for which I had searched.

Then, Frank Ford, president and founder of Arrowhead Mills, and his mother, Lucile, provided the final impetus. After having sampled several of my homemade delights, they put me in touch with Rudy Shur of Avery Publishing. He, too, was convinced my recipes had merit and would make a great cookbook of American classic desserts using natural ingredients. I committed myself to finalizing my ideas on paper in such a way that another person could duplicate my successes.

In the beginning, I knew little about cooking with natural sweeteners, or about oven temperatures, pans, and utensils. But I approached the subject with the same vigor and determination I have approached any subject that captivated my interest. I began to read, research, experiment, and improvise much in the same way I do with my music. Trial and error produced as many failures as successes; but gradually there emerged certain generalizations and principles for cooking with natural sweeteners. Now I can share my sweet successes with you.

Perhaps you, too, have been looking for healthier desserts that are as rich and palatable as those that came from grandmother's kitchen. If so, this book is for you. You will find it simple to use as the recipes are listed in the index under their most general and basic names. The ingredients are also basic; feel free to add creative touches to make the recipes your own.

Hopefully, this collection of recipes will provide a basic repertoire of family favorites that will be enjoyed for its versatility and simple good taste for years to come. Browse through the various sections—Beverages; Pies and Pastries; Cookies; Cakes; Candies, Frostings, Glazes; and Cooling Desserts; you are certain to find your family's favorite as well as a few recipes that bear trying. Each section begins with Hints—ideas on using equipment, avoiding mistakes, creating variations.

Delicious desserts can indeed be made without relying upon overly refined ingredients. Get ready for the compliments you will receive from those who partake of these naturally sweet classic desserts.

Introduction

Strange as it may sound, I have processed white sugar to thank for the writing of this book. Several years ago, I began to suspect that sugar could be linked to allergies, digestive problems, and overall poor health. I knew that dental cavities are attributed to the action of bacteria on sugar, and I began to wonder what sugar does to the rest of the body. The more I read about this sparkling white crystal, the more appalled and angry I became. I read that processed sugar can be linked to all the major degenerative diseases of the body as well as to the body's ability to fight infection. White, processed flour proved to be no better. Nutrients are removed from sugar and flour in their processing. Once in the body, white sugar and white flour leach these very same nutrients from the body as they make their way through the digestive system.

I was also surprised to learn that brown sugar is not as healthy as I once thought. Brown sugar is simply molasses mixed with white sugar; a misguided attempt to right a wrong.

In addition, I found that the chemical aspartame found in some artificial sweeteners may also be linked to health problems. Although the long-term effects of this chemical are unclear, it seems that aspartame, with time and heat, changes its form to methyl alcohol (wood alcohol). Methyl alcohol is poisonous to a human being; in a person's body, it changes to formaldehyde. Although the amounts are miniscule, the fact that aspartame is labeled an "artificial" sweetener is enough reason for me to avoid it and those products that contain it.

What You Should Know About Natural Sweeteners

All of the recipes in this book call for natural ingredients. The less processed an ingredient is, the more beneficial it will be for your health. This is a basic principle of which those interested in their health are keenly aware. Less understood are the principles guiding the use of natural sweeteners, which were once more commonly used.

Molasses was once a staple of the American kitchen. Unsulphured molasses is made from the juice of sun-ripened sugar cane. It is one of the first products extracted from the sugar cane in the long line of the refining process. Being relatively unprocessed, molasses maintains its basic nutrients such as the B vitamins and iron. Molasses also contains calcium. Best stored at room temperature, molasses has a strong flavor, and I have found it is best suited to spicy, baked desserts such as gingerbread and certain cookies. Several other American classic desserts such as shoo-fly pie and pecan pie rely on molasses for their distinctive flavors. Small amounts of molasses mixed with larger amounts of honey simulate the taste of brown sugar.

Honey, a major sweetening agent since earliest times, is much milder than molasses. It is available throughout the country in various colors and flavors. We reserve the more expensive or exotic varieties for the table and prefer a raw, unfiltered clover honey for cooking and baking. I have found this variety to be mild and subtle enough in flavor to blend with and complement other ingredients. Mild clover honey allows one to savor the sweetness of a dessert without being constantly aware of the source of that sweetness.

Most references say that honey is sweeter than sugar and that you use less honey than sugar in cooking. When sampled on its own, honey is indeed sweeter than an equal amount of sugar; but something seems to happen when honey is combined with other ingredients and cooked or baked. Therefore, to make naturally sweetened desserts as sweet as their sugary counterparts, I use as much or more honey than I would sugar, while reducing the amount of liquid. In short, I allow my family's preference to be my guide.

Honey has interesting reactions to changes in temperature; it will crystallize if the temperature remains at around 60°F for several months. When the glucose in the honey precipitates out of the solution, crystallization occurs. The higher the glucose content, the more likely the honey is to crystallize. Tupelot Sage honey resists crystallization for a longer period of time because it has a high fructose content.

Honey will store best at room temperature. If the honey crystallizes or becomes hard to pour, submerge the jar in a pan of hot water until the honey is thin enough to pour easily. To stop the flow of honey from a jar, turn the jar in a slow, circular motion while pouring. This will cause the honey to flow back into the jar rather than drip down the outside of the container. In recipes that call for both honey and butter or oil, coat the measuring cup or spoon with a little oil before measuring the honey. The honey will slide out of the measuring container with ease.

Because of its reaction to temperature changes, honey is not suitable for cooked candies or frostings. It easily absorbs moisture from the air while it cools and during storage. Candy made with honey will usually be sticky. However, since honey absorbs moisture, baked goods made with it will maintain their freshness and be slow to mold.

The most delicate of sweeteners is pure maple syrup. It is sweeter than sugar, but not as sweet as honey. Of all the natural sweeteners, it has the least nutritional value. Maple syrup contains very small amounts of calcium, phosphorus, sodium, magnesium, potassium, and iron. Nevertheless, it makes up in flavor what it lacks in nutrition. Maple syrup has the distinction of being the most expensive of natural sweeteners. In fact, it has often been called "liquid gold." It takes 30 to 40 gallons of sap from the sugar maple tree to make a single gallon of pure maple syrup.

Syrups are graded A, B, and C depending on the boiling time, sugar content, and temperature. (In commercial operations, sap from the sugar maple tree is "boiled down" at a temperature approximately 70°F above the boiling point of water.) Grade A, the lightest in color, is the highest in quality. For cooking and baking, however, grades B and C are preferable and less expensive. Be sure that "maple syrup" purchased in the grocery store is pure maple syrup and not the far less expensive maple-flavored syrup.

Since our family uses molasses, honey, and pure maple syrup exclusively as sweeteners, it is economical for us to buy these ingredients in bulk. All store well and maintain quality and flavor for long periods of time.

Keep It Healthful

There are several natural ingredients besides sweeteners that should be used in making healthful desserts. These include sea salt rather than common table salt. Most commercial salt has had the trace elements removed to make it whiter and saltier. It has been subjected to tremendous heat and pressure to cause it to crystallize. This also makes the salt slow to dissolve and difficult to digest. In addition, calcium bicarbonate is added to keep the salt dry and easy to pour. Iodine may be added to prevent goiter, but sufficient amounts of iodine can be obtained from eating dark green and yellow vegetables. What is worse is that sugar is added to the salt to stabilize the iodine; therefore, commercial table salt is not pure salt.

On the other hand, the water has been removed from sea salt by solar evaporation. No chemicals have been added or removed. It is, therefore, easier to digest and assimilate. Sea salt is high in minerals such as gold, copper, iron, calcium, and magnesium that are aids to the digestive process. Even though salt makes up only a tiny part of natural desserts, it is important enough for you to select the healthier ingredient.

Carob is a wonderful, healthy alternative to chocolate or cocoa. In fact, it is so flavorful and possesses so many other virtues that it should not be considered simply as a substitute. It should be accepted and valued on its own merit. Carob is naturally sweet with its own gentle, distinctive flavor. It is rich in minerals and calcium and contains no caffeine. Because of the healthy aspects of carob, it has become a staple of our kitchen. When enough sweetener is added to carob powder, it makes wonderful candies and frostings. Besides its powdered form, carob may also be purchased as chips to use in carob chip cookies. The chips also make a healthy snack when mixed with nuts and raisins.

Allergy-prone and lactose-intolerant individuals will be pleased to know that soy margarine may be substituted for butter, and soy milk may be substituted for milk or cream in most of these recipes. Soy products have served as the source of protein in most Eastern countries for centuries. They should not be neglected here. My family was surprised and pleased at the interesting possibilities presented by soy products. Frostings made with soy margarine have a creamy texture and fine flavor. Soy custard is delicious, rich and creamy. Soy "ice cream" has a custard-like quality and enjoyable flavor. It also packs and freezes well for future use.

As you can see, natural ingredients are tasty and versatile. I would encourage you to get back to basic ingredients and enjoy the health benefits that you will reap when cooking with whole grains, natural sweeteners, and other natural ingredients. Natural desserts can be even more appealing than their sugary, processed counterparts.

Cakes

Show off your baking skills with these
great-tasting cakes for all occasions.
You provide the frosting and then let
nature provide the decoration—
fresh garden flowers, mint leaves, whole
fruits, sculptured fruit rinds, and nuts—
a rainbow of natural color.

Hints

❧ Use large eggs for the following cake recipes.

❧ Unsifted flours were measured right from the container without sifting. When using commercially presifted flour, pack the flour tightly in the measuring cup by tapping the bottom of the cup on a hard surface.

❧ Unless otherwise indicated, use all ingredients at room temperature so that they will blend more evenly.

❧ The best oils to use for baking are expeller pressed unrefined corn, sesame, or safflower oil. These can be found in health-food stores.

❧ Test cakes for doneness only when they have risen and have baked for the minimum required time. Insert a toothpick or bamboo skewer near the center of the cake. If no batter clings to the pick, the cake is done.

❧ In order to maintain the moisture in a cake, cover it with a clean kitchen towel while it is cooling. Add 10 minutes to the cooling time.

❧ When frosting bottom layers first, use two large spatulas to move and place the top layers.

❧ Cool cakes completely before frosting. Strips of waxed paper placed on the bottom of the cake plate before frosting and slowly removed afterwards will catch messy spills and make for a more attractive creation.

Select-A-Pan

for Basic Yellow, Coconut, Orange, Carob, German
Carob, Spice, Banana, Carrot, Date, and Apple Cakes

Make sure your pan is well-oiled and floured. Fill the pans no more than half full. Use remaining batter to make cupcakes. The baking times are estimated and may vary according to altitude and individual oven. Test for doneness by inserting a toothpick into center of cake after it has baked for the minimum time required. Cake is done if toothpick is clean when removed.

Pan Size	Approx. Baking Time for 350° Oven
Two 9″ x 1½″ round pans	35 to 40 minutes
One 9″ x 1½″ round pan (half recipe)	30 to 35 minutes
Two 8″ x 8″ x 2″ square pans	30 to 35 minutes
One 8″ x 8″ x 2″ square pan (half recipe)	25 to 30 minutes
One 10″ tube pan	40 to 45 minutes
Two 9″ x 5″ loaf pans*	35 to 40 minutes
One 9″ x 5″ loaf pan (half recipe)	30 to 35 minutes
One 13″ x 9″ x 2″ baking pan	30 to 35 minutes
One 15″ x 10″ x 1″ baking pan	25 to 30 minutes
One 12-cupcake tin (Fill spaces half full with batter, full or half recipe.)**	18 to 23 minutes

*These loaf pans work best for those cakes made with oil (Spice, Banana, Carrot, Date, and Apple cakes). Other cakes tend to split at the top.
**Empty cupcake spaces should be filled halfway with water.

Basic Yellow Cake

Here's the recipe for a basic cake that serves multiple purposes.
Hot water is the secret to its success.

PREPARATION TIME:	20 minutes
BAKING TIME:	40 minutes
COOLING TIME:	30 minutes
YIELD:	12 servings

1½ cups unbleached flour, unsifted
1 cup whole-wheat pastry flour, unsifted
½ teaspoon sea salt
3 teaspoons baking powder
1 cup (2 sticks) butter or soy margarine, melted
1½ cups honey
2 teaspoons vanilla
½ cup hot water
2 whole eggs (large) + 4 yolks (large), room temperature

1. Preheat oven to 350°F.

2. In a medium-sized bowl, sift together the flours, salt, and baking powder. Set aside.

3. In a large bowl, combine butter, honey, vanilla, hot water, eggs, and yolks. Beat thoroughly.

4. Add dry ingredients to liquid mixture. Mix on slow speed until ingredients are thoroughly blended.

5. Beat for 1 minute on high speed.

6. Pour batter into two well-oiled and lightly-floured 9-inch round cake pans.

7. Bake 35–40 minutes or until toothpick inserted near center comes out clean.

8. Cool cake on wire racks for 30 minutes before removing from pans.

9. Cool completely before frosting with Butter Cream, Carob Cream, Divinity, Maple Fudge, Carob Fudge, Peanut Butter Fudge, Whipped Cream, or Fruit Cream-Cheese frostings (see pages 126–140). Fruit spreads can be used on the middle layer for a tasty variation.

Variations

Single-Layer Cake

Cut recipe in half and bake 30–35 minutes.

Yellow Cupcakes

Cut the Basic Yellow Cake recipe in half. Follow directions for mixing. Place paper baking cups in muffin pan. Fill each cup with 2 tablespoons of batter. Bake 18–23 minutes or until tested done. Serve plain or frosted. Makes 18 cupcakes.

Coconut Cake

Follow directions for Basic Yellow Cake. Frost with Divinity Frosting (see page 130). Before assembling cake, sprinkle top, sides, and layers with $1\frac{1}{2}$ cups shredded or flaked, unsweetened coconut.

Orange Cake

Follow directions for Basic Yellow Cake. Replace the vanilla with orange extract. Add 2 teaspoons grated orange peel. Frost with Cream Cheese Frosting (see page 130), substituting orange extract for vanilla and adding a teaspoon of grated orange peel.

Carob Cake

A great rival for chocolate that will please your palatte.
It's moist, rich, and tender.

PREPARATION TIME: 20 minutes
BAKING TIME: 40 minutes
YIELD: 12 servings

1½ *cups unbleached flour, unsifted*
⅔ *cup whole-wheat pastry flour, unsifted*
¼ *cup carob powder*
½ *teaspoon sea salt*
3 teaspoons baking powder
1 cup (2 sticks) butter or soy margarine, melted
1½ *cups honey*
2 teaspoons vanilla
½ *cup hot water*
2 whole eggs + 4 yolks (large), room temperature

1. Preheat oven to 350°F.

2. In a medium-sized bowl, sift together the flours, carob, salt, and baking powder. Set aside.

3. In a large bowl, combine butter, honey, vanilla, hot water, eggs, and yolks. Beat thoroughly.

4. Add the dry ingredients to the liquid mixture.

5. Mix on slow speed until thoroughly blended.

6. Beat for 1 minute on high speed.

7. Pour batter into 2 well-oiled and lightly-floured 9-inch round cake pans.

8. Bake 35–40 minutes or until toothpick inserted near center comes out clean.

9. Cool cake on wire racks for 30 minutes.

10. Cool completely before frosting with Carob Cream, Carob Mint, Whipped Cream, or Divinity frostings (see pages 130–138).

Variations

One-Layer Cake

For a single layer cake, cut recipe in half and bake 30–35 minutes.

Carob Cupcakes

Cut the Two-Layer Carob Cake recipe in half. Follow directions for mixing. Place paper baking cups in muffin pan. Place 2 tablespoons of batter in each cup. Bake 18–23 minutes or until tested done. Serve plain or frosted. Makes 18 cupcakes.

German Carob Cake

Follow directions for Carob Cake. Frost with Pecan Frosting (see page 139).

Carrot Cake

What a delicious trio: carrots, dates, and apples!
Make two loaves and freeze one for a busy day.

PREPARATION TIME:	20 minutes
BAKING TIME:	35–45 minutes
COOLING TIME:	30 minutes
YIELD:	12–15 servings

4 large eggs, room temperature
1¼ cups honey
⅔ cup cooking oil
1 cup whole-wheat pastry flour, unsifted
1 cup unbleached flour, unsifted
2½ teaspoons baking powder
1 teaspoon sea salt
2 teaspoons cinnamon
2 cups finely grated carrots

1. Preheat oven to 350°F.

2. Beat together eggs, honey, and oil in a large mixing bowl.

3. Add dry ingredients and the carrots. Mix thoroughly.

4. Pour into 2 well-oiled and floured 9-inch x 5-inch loaf pans and bake for 35–40 minutes or pour into a 10-inch fluted tube pan and bake for 40–45 minutes.

5. Cool cake 30 minutes on a rack.

6. Serve plain or with Cream Cheese Frosting (see page 130).

Variations

Carrot Cupcakes

Prepare Carrot Cake through step 3. Place 2 tablespoons of batter in each cupcake tin and bake at 350°F for 18–23 minutes. A full recipe will yield 24 cupcakes, a half-recipe, 12 cupcakes.

Date Cake

Follow the recipe for Carrot Cake except substitute 2 cups of finely chopped pitted dates for the carrots. Beat until dates are well blended into the batter.

Apple Cake

Follow the recipe for carrot cake except substitute 2 cups of peeled, coarsely grated apples for the carrots.

Spice Cake

The perfect combination of spices.

PREPARATION TIME:	20 minutes
BAKING TIME:	35–40 minutes
COOLING TIME:	1 hour or until cake is room temperature
YIELD:	10–12 servings

$^2\!/_3$ *cup oil*
$1^1\!/_4$ *cups honey*
4 large eggs, room temperature
$^2\!/_3$ *cup unsweetened applesauce*
1 cup whole-wheat pastry flour, unsifted
1 cup unbleached flour, unsifted
$2^1\!/_2$ *teaspoons baking powder*
$^1\!/_2$ *teaspoon sea salt*
1 teaspoon cinnamon
$^1\!/_2$ *teaspoon nutmeg*
$^1\!/_2$ *teaspoon ground cloves*
1 cup nuts, chopped (optional)

1. Preheat oven to 350°F.

2. In a large bowl, beat together oil, honey, eggs, and applesauce until ingredients are well blended.

3. Add the remaining ingredients and mix until batter is smooth.

4. Turn into a well-oiled and floured 13-inch x 9-inch baking pan.

5. Bake for 30–35 minutes or until a toothpick inserted in the center comes out clean. (May also be baked in a 10-inch fluted tube pan for 40 minutes.)

6. Serve plain or with Butter Cream Frosting (see page 135) topped with nuts.

Variations

Banana Cake

Follow the recipe for Spice Cake except replace the applesauce with mashed bananas; eliminate the spices and add 2 teaspoons vanilla.

Spice Cupcakes

Prepare batter for either Spice or Banana cake. Place paper baking cups in muffin pan. Fill each with 2 tablespoons of batter. Bake at 350°F for 18–23 minutes. Remove cupcakes from the pan while they are still warm. Cool them on a rack. Frost when completely cooled. A full recipe makes 24 cupcakes. The recipe may be halved and will yield 12 cupcakes.

Gingerbread

*There's nothing like warm, spicy gingerbread on a cold day.
Delicious topped with a scoop of vanilla ice cream.*

PREPARATION TIME: 15 minutes
BAKING TIME: 40 minutes
YIELD: 6 servings

½ cup (1 stick) butter or soy margarine, melted
½ cup honey
½ cup molasses
½ cup hot water
2 large egg yolks, beaten, room temperature
¾ cup whole-wheat pastry flour, unsifted
¾ cup unbleached flour, unsifted
½ teaspoon baking powder
¼ teaspoon sea salt
½ teaspoon ginger
½ teaspoon cinnamon

1. Preheat oven to 350°F.

2. Combine butter, honey, molasses, hot water, and beaten egg yolks. Beat thoroughly. Set aside.

3. Sift together dry ingredients and mix with liquid mixture.

4. Pour batter into a well-oiled and floured 8-inch x 8-inch x 2-inch pan.

5. Bake 35–40 minutes or until toothpick inserted near center comes out clean.

6. Serve warm with Lemon Sauce (see page 142) or whipped cream.

Variation

Gingerbread Cupcakes

Place paper baking cups in muffin pan. Fill each with 2 tablespoons of batter. Bake at 350°F for 18–23 minutes. This recipe will yield 16 cupcakes.

Boston Cream Pie

*The parts go together as in a cake,
but in New England, "pie" is its traditional name.*

PREPARATION TIME:	25 minutes
BAKING TIME:	40 minutes
COOLING TIME:	1 hour
YIELD:	12 servings

*1 Vanilla Cream Pudding recipe (see page 107), chilled and firmly set.
½ Basic Yellow Cake recipe (see page 8)
½ Carob Cream Frosting recipe (see page 138)*

1. Bake the Basic Yellow Cake in an oiled and floured 9-inch cake pan for 30–35 minutes or until tested done.

2. Cool cake for 30 minutes before removing from pan.

3. Cool completely before cutting into 2 layers.

4. Spread Vanilla Cream Pudding between layers.

5. Frost with ½ Carob Cream Frosting recipe.

Pineapple Upside-Down Cake

A bright, tasty cake that you'll be proud to serve.

PREPARATION TIME:	25 minutes
BAKING TIME:	35 minutes
COOLING TIME:	30 minutes
YIELD:	8 servings

Cake Batter

½ cup (1 stick) butter or soy margarine, melted
¾ cup honey
1 teaspoon vanilla
2 large eggs
¼ cup milk or soy milk, room temperature
1 cup unbleached flour, unsifted
¼ cup whole-wheat pastry flour, unsifted
1 teaspoon baking powder
¼ teaspoon sea salt

Topping

3 tablespoons butter or soy margarine
¼ cup honey
2 teaspoons molasses
4 slices unsweetened pineapple (7-ounce can, drained)
pecan halves for decoration

1. Preheat oven to 350°F.

2. In a medium-sized bowl, combine first 5 ingredients and beat until foamy.

3. Sift remaining dry ingredients into liquid mixture and beat until batter is smooth. Set aside.

4. Line the sides and bottom of a 9-inch cake pan with a single sheet of wax paper.

5. Arrange slices of pineapple and pecans on the bottom. Set aside.

6. Prepare the topping by melting the butter, honey, and molasses in a saucepan over medium heat.

7. Gently pour this liquid topping over the pineapple.

8. Spread the cake batter evenly over the topping layer.

9. Bake for 30–35 minutes or until toothpick inserted in the center comes out clean.

10. Cool cake in pan for 30 minutes.

11. Invert pan, remove cake from pan, and carefully peel off wax paper.

Pound Cake

Plain and simple with a rich, buttery flavor.

PREPARATION TIME:	25 minutes
BAKING TIME:	70 minutes
COOLING TIME:	1 hour
YIELD:	10–12 servings

¾ cup (1½ sticks) butter or soy margarine
1 cup honey
2 teaspoons vanilla
1 cup unbleached flour, unsifted
½ cup whole-wheat pastry flour, unsifted
¼ teaspoon sea salt
½ teaspoon baking powder
½ teaspoon nutmeg
1 whole egg (large) + 3 yolks (large), beaten,
room temperature

1. Preheat oven to 300°F.

2. Cream butter, honey, and vanilla in a large bowl.

3. Sift flours, salt, and baking powder into the mixture.

4. Add nutmeg and mix thoroughly until batter is smooth.

5. Add whole egg and yolks and beat for 3 minutes at high speed while scrapping the sides of the bowl with a rubber spatula.

6. Pour batter into a well-oiled and floured 9-inch x 5-inch loaf pan.

7. Bake for 65–70 minutes. Do not test for doneness until cake has risen and split. A toothpick inserted into the center should come out dry and clean.

8. Cool the cake on a rack until it can be handled.

9. Remove cake from pan and cool to room temperature.

10. Wrap in aluminum foil to keep cake moist.

11. Serve plain or with fruit.

Angel Food Cake

*This unbelievably light and fluffy cake is perfect
for elegant entertaining. It's a great way to use
those egg whites you've been saving.*

PREPARATON TIME:	35 minutes
BAKING TIME:	23 minutes
COOLING TIME:	2 hours
YIELD:	12–15 servings

*¾ cup honey
1 cup unbleached flour, unsifted
1½ cups egg whites (12–14 egg whites)
¼ teaspoon sea salt
1 teaspoon vanilla
¼ cup pure maple syrup**

1. Preheat oven to 425°F.

2. Warm the honey to thin it, and then allow it to come to room temperature.

3. Bring all ingredients to room temperature.

4. Sift flour 6 times. Set aside.

5. Place an ungreased 10-inch tube pan in the oven until batter is mixed.

6. Beat egg whites until they are glossy and foamy.

7. Add salt and continue beating until egg whites stand in peaks.

8. Add vanilla, honey, and maple syrup. Beat until batter is evenly mixed.

9. Sift the flour, small amounts at a time, onto the mixture. Fold and cut through the mixture with a rubber spatula after each addition. Do not beat.

10. Spoon the mixture into the pre-heated pan and smooth the top with a spatula.

11. Bake the cake undisturbed for 23 minutes. Top will be dark brown.

12. Remove cake from oven and invert pan immediately.

13. Cool cake to room temperature.

14. Run a sharp knife around the outside and inside edges of the cake pan.

15. Lift the cake out of the pan by gripping the central core. Run a knife under the cake to free it.

16. Serve plain or with pudding, Lemon Sauce (see page 142), Carob Syrup (see page 144), Whipped Cream Frosting (see page 137), or Fruit Cream Cheese Frosting (see page 140).

---

*You may substitute ¼ cup of honey for the maple syrup.

Fruit Cake

*Greet the holiday season with an unbelievable fruit cake.
It's bound to make new converts to this famous dessert,
so make more than one.*

PREPARATION TIME: 45 minutes
BAKING TIME: 65–70 minutes
YIELD: 12–15 servings

½ cup unbleached white flour, unsifted
¼ cup whole-wheat pastry flour, unsifted
¼ teaspoon sea salt
½ teaspoon baking powder
½ cup raisins, minced
½ cup pitted dates, minced
1 cup diced, dried pears or apples
1 cup diced, dried pineapple
1½ cups chopped nuts
3 large eggs, room temperature
½ cup honey
¼ cup molasses or pure maple syrup, room temperature
1 teaspoon vanilla extract
½ teaspoon almond extract

1. Preheat oven to 300°F and place a pan of water on the bottom shelf.

2. Mix all dry ingredients, fruits, and nuts together in a large bowl and set aside.

3. In a medium-sized bowl, beat the eggs, honey, molasses, and extracts until they are foamy.

4. Add the liquid mixture to the dry mixture and stir with a wooden spoon until batter is well blended.

5. Spoon into a well-oiled ring pan and bake for 65–70 minutes or until a toothpick inserted near the center comes out clean.

Variation

Mini Fruit Cakes

Spoon batter into a well-oiled muffin tin. Bake 35–45 minutes. Cool cakes on a rack. Wrap tightly in foil and/or a damp cloth and refrigerate.

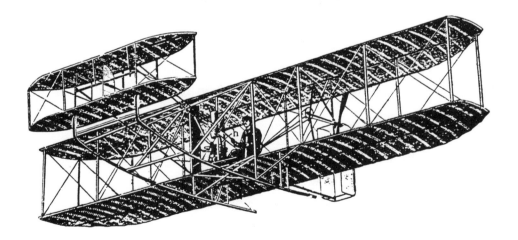

Crumb Cake (Streusel)

Pour a cup of your favorite hot brew and enjoy some old-fashioned goodness.

PREPARATION TIME:	20 minutes
BAKING TIME:	35 minutes
YIELD:	8–10 servings

Cake Batter
1 cup whole-wheat pastry flour, unsifted
½ cup unbleached flour, unsifted
¼ teaspoon sea salt
1 teaspoon baking powder
⅓ cup oil
¾ cup honey
1 large egg, beaten, room temperature
¼ cup milk or soy milk, room temperature

Topping
¼ cup whole-wheat pastry flour, unsifted
1 teaspoon cinnamon
4 tablespoons butter or soy margarine
½ cup nuts, chopped
¼ cup molasses, pure maple syrup,
or Maple Sugar (see page 132)

1. Preheat oven to 375°F.

2. In a large bowl, stir together the dry cake batter ingredients until they are blended.

3. Gradually add the liquids, mixing well after each addition.

4. Beat with a wooden spoon until batter is smooth.

5. Pour batter into an oiled 10-inch x $1\frac{1}{2}$-inch pie plate or a 9-inch x 9-inch x 2-inch baking pan.

6. To make the topping, combine the flour and cinnamon. Cut in the butter until crumbly.

7. Sprinkle topping over the batter.

8. Top with nuts and drizzle with molasses, pure maple syrup, or Maple Sugar.

9. Bake 30–35 minutes or until toothpick inserted near center comes out clean.

10. Serve warm.

Variation

Date Crumb Cake

Follow Crumb Cake recipe except add $\frac{1}{2}$ cup chopped or snipped pitted dates to the batter.

Trifle

Trifle is an economical way to use up dry cake or cookies,
but it's attractive and tasty enough for guests.
Make it in a glass baking dish or
individual dessert dishes for the best effect.
Our favorite quick trifle calls for Angel Cake and Lemon Pudding.

PREPARATION TIME:	35 minutes
CHILLING TIME:	$1\frac{1}{2}$ hours
YIELD:	8–10 one-cup servings

$\frac{1}{4}$ *Angel Food Cake (see page 22) sliced into*
$\frac{1}{2}$ *-inch thick pieces or 10–12 cookies*
1 pudding recipe (any flavor on pages 107–113)
1 cup ($\frac{1}{2}$-pint carton) heavy cream
$\frac{1}{2}$ *cup nuts, chopped*

1. Prepare pudding according to directions. Cool to room temperature.

2. Arrange cake or cookies along the bottom of 2-quart glass baking dish.

3. Cover cake or cookies with a layer of pudding.

4. Whip the cream until it is firm, and use half of it to cover the pudding.

5. Sprinkle with half the nuts.

6. Repeat steps 4 and 5.

7. Chill for 1 hour before serving.

Shortcakes

Don't neglect this delectable cake. It's the perfect companion for fresh fruits in season.

PREPARATION TIME: 20 minutes
BAKING TIME: 10–15 minutes
YIELD: 6–8 servings

1 cup whole-wheat pastry flour, unsifted
1¼ cups unbleached flour, unsifted
2 teaspoons baking powder
½ teaspoon sea salt
½ cup (1 stick) butter or soy margarine
¼ cup honey
2 large eggs, beaten, room temperature
2 tablespoons milk or soy milk, room temperature

1. Preheat oven to 450°F.

2. In a medium-sized bowl, combine the dry ingredients.

3. Cut in butter with a pastry blender or two knives.

4. Add honey, eggs, and milk. Blend with a wooden spoon and stir until dough pulls away from the sides of the bowl. Dough will be sticky.

5. Turn dough out on a well-floured surface.

6. Pat or roll to a ½-inch thickness.

7. Cut with a large biscuit cutter or water tumbler for individual cakes.

8. Bake 8–10 minutes on an oiled cookie sheet.

9. Remove cakes from oven and cool before splitting cakes into 2 layers.

10. Spoon honey-sweetened fruit or prepared Fruit Glaze (see page 141) between the layers. Top with fruit and whipped cream.

Variation

Large Shortcake

Spread dough in a well-oiled round cake pan. Bake 12–15 minutes or until golden brown. Follow the procedure for individual shortcakes.

Cheesecake

Sumptuous and creamy; keeps its fine texture
for three to four days in the refrigerator.
Make it a few days ahead for your next party.

ADVANCED PREPARATION:	30 minutes
PREPARATION TIME:	30 minutes
BAKING TIME:	35 minutes
YIELD:	8–10 servings

1 unbaked, 9-inch Crumb Shell (see page 70) or
1 Partially-Baked Pie Shell (see page 76)
12 ounces of cream cheese (1½ eight-ounce packages or
4 three-ounce packages), room temperature
¾ cup sour cream, room temperature
½ cup honey
1 whole egg + 1 egg yolk (large), room temperature
⅛ teaspoon sea salt
¼ teaspoon lemon juice
½ teaspoon vanilla
¼ teaspoon almond extract
1½ tablespoons butter, melted

1. If you are using an unbaked Crumb Shell, refrigerate it for at least 30 minutes before adding the filling.

2. Preheat oven to 325°F.

3. In a large bowl, beat together the cream cheese and sour cream until they are smooth and free of lumps.

4. Add the honey and beat slightly.

5. Add whole egg and egg yolk and beat just to mix.

6. Add the remaining ingredients and beat again until batter is evenly mixed. Do not overbeat.

7. Pour batter into shell and bake on the middle rack of the oven for 35 minutes. Turn off the oven, open the door, and pull out the middle rack as far as it will go. (If small cracks appear near the edges of the cheesecake, they will usually close during proper cooling. Rapid cooling can cause large cracks to form in the center of the cake.) Allow the cake to cool slowly, undisturbed, for 1 hour.

9. Refrigerate for 3 hours before serving.

10. Top with fruit or Fruit Glaze (see page 141) or serve plain.

Cake Doughnuts

*These are a lot easier to make than you would guess.
Surprise your family with a healthy rendition of an old-time favorite.
Frost and freeze for a future delight.*

PREPARATION TIME:	45 minutes
CHILLING TIME:	$1\frac{1}{2}$ hours
FRYING TIME:	6 minutes, approximately
YIELD:	15–20 doughnuts and doughnut holes

$2\frac{1}{4}$ cups whole-wheat pastry flour, unsifted
2 teaspoons baking powder
$\frac{1}{4}$ teaspoon sea salt
$\frac{1}{2}$ teaspoon nutmeg
2 large eggs, beaten, room temperature
$\frac{3}{4}$ cup honey
1 teaspoon vanilla
$\frac{1}{2}$ cup milk or soy milk, room temperature
$\frac{1}{4}$ cup butter or soy margarine, melted
1 cup unbleached flour, unsifted

1. In a medium-sized bowl, stir together the whole-wheat pastry flour, baking powder, salt, and nutmeg. Set aside.

2. In a large bowl, combine eggs, honey, and vanilla. Beat until foamy.

3. Add milk and butter or soy margarine. Stir until blended.

4. Add the whole-wheat mixture to the liquid mixture and beat with an electric mixer until thoroughly blended.

5. Add the unbleached flour and stir with a wooden spoon until batter is evenly blended.

6. Cover the bowl with plastic wrap and chill $1\frac{1}{2}$ hours.

7. On a well-floured surface, roll the dough to $\frac{1}{2}$-inch thickness. Use flour liberally as dough will be sticky.

8. Cut with a floured $2\frac{1}{2}$-inch doughnut cutter. Reroll as needed. If dough becomes too limp, refrigerate before proceeding.

9. Fry 2 or 3 doughnuts at a time in deep, hot oil (375°F) for about 1 minute on each side or until doughnuts are golden brown.

10. Drain on paper towels.

11. Serve warm; frost with $\frac{1}{2}$ recipe of Carob Cream Frosting (see page 138) or Butter Cream Frosting (see page 135).

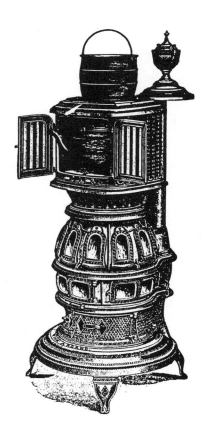

Jelly Roll

Nothing's prettier than a jelly roll!
You'll get many requests for this family favorite,
and the variations are nearly unlimited.

PREPARATION TIME: 25 minutes
BAKING TIME: 12 minutes
YIELD: 6–8 servings

Batter

4 large eggs, separated, room temperature
½ cup honey
1½ teaspoons vanilla
⅓ cup whole-wheat pastry flour, unsifted
⅓ cup unbleached flour, unsifted
¼ teaspoon sea salt
1 teaspoon baking powder

Filling

Any of the following:
Butter Cream Frosting (see page 135)
Carob Cream Frosting (see page 138)
Divinity Frosting (see page 130)
Maple Cream Frosting (see page 136)
sugarless jelly
whipped cream

Figure 1. Roll cake in jelly roll style. Begin with one of the short sides. Place towel under cake for ease in handling.

1. Preheat oven to 375°F.

2. Oil and flour a 10-inch x 15-inch x 1-inch jelly roll pan. Set aside.

3. In a medium-sized bowl, beat the egg whites on high speed until they form soft peaks. Set aside.

4. In a large bowl, beat the egg yolks, honey, and vanilla until they are well mixed.

5. Sift the flours, salt, and baking powder into the mixture and beat until smooth and evenly mixed.

6. Beat in the egg whites until they are well blended.

7. Pour batter into jelly roll pan. Tilt pan until batter is evenly distributed.

8. Bake 10–12 minutes until top is lightly browned. Do not overbake.

9. Remove pan from oven and use a spatula to loosen the edges and bottom of the cake while it is still warm.

10. Cool cake slightly.

11. Spread filling evenly over the surface.

12. Roll cake in jelly roll style beginning with one of the short sides. (See illustration on page 36.)

13. Place on a cake plate, seam down.

14. To retain moisture, cover cake with a damp paper towel or cloth until ready to serve.

Variation

Yule Log

Fill Jelly Roll with sugarless jelly, roll as above, and frost with Carob Cream Frosting (see page 138). Score the log with the tines of a fork to simulate bark. Garnish with holly sprigs.

Ice Cream Sandwich Cake

*The most sumptuous combinations are German Carob Cake
with Vanilla Ice Cream and Pecan Frosting,
Yellow Cake with any flavor ice cream and
Carob or Maple Cream frosting.*

PREPARATION TIME:	40 minutes
BAKING TIME:	35 minutes
COOLING TIME:	60 minutes
YIELD:	8–10 servings

*1 quart ice cream (see page 153) or
soy ice cream (see page 155), any flavor
$\frac{1}{2}$ cake recipe (any flavor)
$\frac{1}{2}$ recipe Carob Cream, Maple Cream, Whipped Cream,
or Pecan frosting (see pages 136–139)*

1. Preheat oven to 350°F.

2. Line a 9-inch round cake pan with plastic wrap.

3. Pack softened ice cream into the pan and refreeze until it is firm.

4. Prepare $\frac{1}{2}$ a cake recipe to make a single-layer cake.

5. Bake in an oiled and floured 9-inch cake pan for 30–35 minutes or until tested done.

6. Cool cake completely for 1 hour before removing from the pan.

7. Prepare the frosting while the cake is cooling. Set aside.

8. Slice the single layer in half to create two thinner layers.

9. Remove the ice cream from the pan and sandwich it between the 2 halves of the layer cake.

10. Frost and serve immediately.

Pudding Cake

Make the pudding a day ahead so it has a chance to set.
Once that's done, this winning recipe goes together quickly.

PREPARATION TIME:	25 minutes
BAKING TIME:	40 minutes
COOLING TIME:	1 hour
YIELD:	12 servings

1 Vanilla Cream Pudding recipe (see page 107), chilled and firmly set
1 Basic Yellow Cake (recipe on page 8)
¼ cup poppy seeds
½ Whipped Cream Frosting recipe (see page 137)
1 cup slivered almonds
¼ cup Carob Syrup (recipe on page 144)

1. Prepare batter for Basic Yellow Cake, adding poppy seeds just before beating in eggs.

2. Bake the cake as directed and let it cool completely.

3. Spread Vanilla Cream Pudding between layers.

4. Frost top and sides with Whipped Cream Frosting and sprinkle with almonds.

5. Drizzle Carob Syrup on top.

Baked Alaska

Try this beautiful dessert when the occasion calls for cake and ice cream.
This Texas flatland version is more practical
and easier to put together than the original.
To cut down even more on the preparation time,
use ice cream that was previously made and frozen.

PREPARATION TIME:	40 minutes
BAKING TIME:	35 minutes
COOLING TIME:	60 minutes
YIELD:	8–10 servings

1 quart ice cream (see page 153)
or soy milk ice cream (see page 155), any flavor
½ cake recipe, any flavor
6 egg whites
1 tablespoon honey or pure maple syrup

1. Preheat oven to 350°F.

2. Line a 9-inch round cake pan with plastic wrap.

3. Pack softened ice cream into the pan and refreeze until it is firm.

4. Prepare ½ a cake recipe to make a single-layer cake.

5. Bake in an oiled and floured 9-inch cake pan for 30–35 minutes or until tested done.

6. Cool cake completely for about 1 hour before removing from the pan.

7. Preheat the oven to 500°F.

8. Slice the single layer in half to create 2 thinner layers.

9. Remove the ice cream from the pan and sandwich it between the 2 halves of the layer cake.

10. Return all to the freezer.

11. Beat the 6 egg whites and honey until soft peaks (meringue) form.

12. Transfer the cake to a baking sheet.

13. Spread the meringue over all, sealing the edges of the meringue to the baking sheet.

14. Place on the lowest rack in the oven for 2–3 minutes or until peaks are golden.

15. Serve immediately.

Cookies

Your cookie jar is waiting to be filled with
these truly American snack-desserts.
Flavor and shape these classic treats
for those special holiday times
and for all those in-between times.

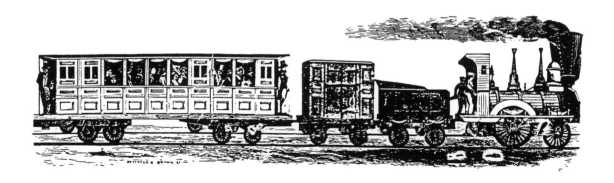

Hints

❧ These recipes call for unsifted flour. When using commercially pre-sifted flour, pack the flour tightly in the measuring cup by tapping the bottom of the measuring cup on a hard surface.

❧ The dough for drop-cookies tends to spread more than rolled cookie dough when baked. To prevent its spreading too much, drop the dough on cool baking sheets. Allow baking sheets that come directly from the oven to cool for several minutes before reusing. Leave 2 inches between cookies to allow for spread.

❧ To avoid rolled dough's sticking to cookie cutters, dust the cutters with flour before using them.

❧ Keep the dough for rolled cookies covered and chilled until you are ready to use it.

❧ Those cookies made with butter or soy margarine can be frozen up to six months. To ensure the best quality, be sure to completely cool the cookies before wrapping them individually.

Vanilla Cookies

Crunchy cookies for the lunch box, break time, or holiday festivities. All variations freeze well and retain their flavor for up to six months.

PREPARATION TIME:	20 minutes
BAKING TIME:	8–10 minutes
COOLING TIME:	10 minutes
YIELD:	$2\frac{1}{2}$ dozen

$\frac{1}{2}$ *cup (1 stick) butter or soy margarine, melted*
$\frac{1}{2}$ *cup honey*
1 teaspoon vanilla
$1\frac{1}{4}$ *cups unbleached flour, unsifted*
$\frac{1}{4}$ *teaspoon baking powder*
$\frac{1}{4}$ *teaspoon sea salt*

1. Preheat oven to 350°F.

2. In a medium-sized bowl, beat butter, honey, and vanilla together.

3. Sift the dry ingredients into the liquid mixture.

4. Beat until smooth.

5. Drop by $\frac{1}{2}$ teaspoons onto an oiled cookie sheet.

6. Bake for 8–10 minutes or until cookies are brown around the edges.

7. Remove cookies from oven and cool on a rack.

Variations

Lemon Cookies

Follow the recipe for Vanilla Cookies except eliminate vanilla and replace with $\frac{1}{2}$ teaspoon lemon extract.

Orange Cookies

Follow the recipe for Vanilla Cookies except eliminate vanilla and replace with $\frac{1}{2}$ teaspoon orange extract.

Mint Cookies

Follow the recipe for Vanilla Cookies except eliminate vanilla and replace with $\frac{1}{2}$ teaspoon peppermint extract.

Carob Cookies

Rich-tasting enough to rival the chocolate variety.

PREPARATION TIME:	20 minutes
BAKING TIME:	8–10 minutes
COOLING TIME:	20 minutes
YIELD:	3 dozen

½ cup (1 stick) butter or soy margarine, melted
¾ cup honey
½ teaspoon vanilla
¾ cup unbleached flour, unsifted
½ cup whole-wheat pastry flour, unsifted
2 tablespoons carob powder
¼ teaspoon baking powder
¼ teaspoon sea salt
½ cup nuts, chopped

1. Preheat oven to 350°F.

2. In a medium-sized bowl, beat butter, honey, and vanilla together.

3. Sift dry ingredients into liquid mixture.

4. Beat until smooth.

5. Stir in nuts.

6. Drop batter by ½ teaspoons onto an oiled cookie sheet.

7. Bake for 8–10 minutes or until bottoms of cookies are brown.

8. Remove cookies from oven and cool on a rack.

Variation

Carob Mint Cookies

Follow directions for Carob Cookies except substitute peppermint extract for vanilla.

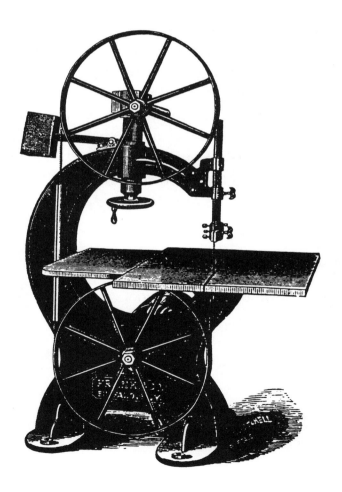

Gingerbread Cutouts

The cookies to bring back memories.

PREPARATION TIME: 25 minutes
BAKING TIME: 5–7 minutes
COOLING TIME: 10 minutes
YIELD: 2–3 dozen

$\frac{3}{4}$ *cup whole-wheat pastry flour, unsifted*
$1\frac{1}{4}$ *cups unbleached flour, unsifted*
$\frac{1}{4}$ *teaspoon sea salt*
$\frac{1}{2}$ *teaspoon ginger*
$\frac{1}{2}$ *teaspoon cinnamon*
$\frac{1}{2}$ *cup (1 stick) butter or soy margarine, melted*
$\frac{1}{2}$ *cup molasses*

1. Preheat oven to 375°F.

2. Combine all dry ingredients in a large bowl and mix well.

3. Add butter and molasses and stir with a wooden spoon until dough pulls away from the sides of the bowl.

4. Shape dough into a ball with floured hands.

5. Flatten ball on floured surface.

6. Sprinkle top of ball with flour and roll out to $\frac{1}{8}$-inch thickness.

7. Cut with $4\frac{1}{2}$-inch to 6-inch cutters. (Dough scraps may be reshaped into a ball and the process repeated.)

8. Place cookies on unoiled cookie sheet and pierce several times with a fork.

9. Bake 5–7 minutes or until cookies are lightly browned on the edges. Watch carefully and do not overbake.

10. Cool cookies on a rack.

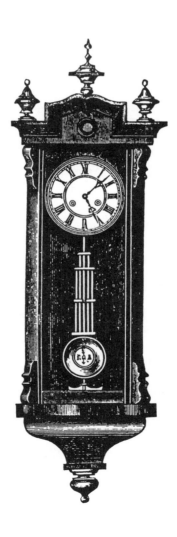

Maple Sugar Cookies

Without a doubt, our family favorite. The flavor is delicate—perfect with milk or a cup of herb tea.

PREPARATION TIME:	20 minutes
BAKING TIME:	8–10 minutes
COOLING TIME:	10 minutes
YIELD:	2 dozen

1½ cups unbleached flour, unsifted
¼ teaspoon sea salt
½ cup (1 stick) butter or soy margarine, melted
⅓ cup pure maple syrup
1 tablespoon Maple Sugar (see page 132), optional

1. Preheat oven to 375°F.

2. Combine flour, salt, butter, and syrup in a medium-sized bowl.

3. Stir with a wooden spoon until dough pulls away from the sides of the bowl.

4. Shape dough into a ball with your hands.

5. Roll out ⅛-inch thick on a floured surface.

6. Cut with biscuit or cookie cutters to desired shapes. (Dough scraps may be reshaped into a ball and the process repeated.)

7. Place cookies on an unoiled cookie sheet.

8. Bake for 8–10 minutes or until cookies are lightly browned around the edges. Watch carefully and do not overbake.

9. Cool cookies on a rack. If desired, brush tops lightly with water then sprinkle with Maple Sugar.

Graham Crackers

Fall in love with this famous cracker.
Be sure to bake extra and freeze for use
in the best possible crumb crust.

PREPARATION TIME:	20 minutes
BAKING TIME:	8–10 minutes
COOLING TIME:	10 minutes
YIELD:	$2\frac{1}{2}$ dozen

$1\frac{1}{2}$ *cups whole-wheat pastry flour, unsifted*
$1\frac{1}{2}$ *cups unbleached flour, unsifted*
1 teaspoon baking powder
$\frac{1}{2}$ *teaspoon sea salt*
$\frac{1}{2}$ *cup honey*
$\frac{1}{3}$ *cup molasses*
$\frac{1}{2}$ *cup (1 stick) butter or soy margarine, melted*
1 large egg, beaten, room temperature

1. Preheat oven to 375°F.

2. In a large bowl, combine all the dry ingredients and mix well.

3. Add the liquid ingredients and stir vigorously until ingredients are blended.

4. Divide the dough in half and form a ball with your hands.

5. Dust the ball of dough lightly with flour and roll to about $\frac{1}{8}$-inch thickness.

6. Cut into rectangular or square shapes and use a spatula to transfer shapes to an unoiled cookie sheet.

7. Pierce shapes with a fork several times for air vents and decoration.

8. Bake for 8–10 minutes or until crackers are lightly browned around the edges.

9. Cool crackers on a rack.

Meringue Cookies

The most delicate of all cookies.

PREPARATION TIME:	10 minutes
BAKING TIME:	55 minutes
COOLING TIME:	10 minutes
YIELD:	2 dozen

2 large egg whites
¼ cup pure maple syrup
¼ teaspoon vanilla extract
⅓ cup almonds, ground, optional

1. Preheat oven to 275°F.

2. Line a cookie sheet with aluminum foil or brown, unglazed paper.

3. Beat egg whites until soft peaks form.

4. Add maple syrup gradually and continue to beat until soft peaks reform.

5. Fold in vanilla and, if desired, finely ground almonds.

6. Drop batter by teaspoons onto baking sheet and bake for 45 minutes.

7. Reduce heat to 250°F and continue baking for an additional 10 minutes.

8. Allow cookies to completely cool before carefully peeling them off of the foil.

Brownies

Our version of a supreme classic.

PREPARATION TIME:	10 minutes
BAKING TIME:	25–30 minutes
COOLING TIME:	1 hour
YIELD:	2 dozen

½ cup (1 stick) butter or soy margarine, melted
1¼ cups honey
2 teaspoons vanilla
1 cup whole-wheat pastry flour, unsifted
⅓ cup carob powder, sifted
½ teaspoon sea salt
⅓ cup milk or soy milk, room temperature
2 large eggs, beaten, room temperature
1 cup nuts, chopped.

1. Preheat oven to 350°F.

2. Combine butter, honey, vanilla, flour, carob powder, and salt. Mix well.

3. Beat in milk, eggs, and nuts.

4. Pour into a well-oiled 9-inch x 13-inch baking dish.

5. Bake for 25–30 minutes or until toothpick inserted in the middle comes out clean.

6. Cool for an hour before cutting into 24 brownies.

Variations

Double Fudge Brownies

Prepare $\frac{1}{2}$ recipe of Carob Cream Frosting (see page 138). Spread over Brownies before serving.

Peanut Butter Brownies

Follow the recipe for Brownies except decrease carob powder to $\frac{1}{4}$ cup. Add $\frac{1}{2}$ cup natural smooth peanut butter after adding honey.

Macaroons

Crisp on the outside and chewy on the inside.

PREPARATION TIME:	10 minutes
BAKING TIME:	10–15 minutes
COOLING TIME:	10 minutes
YIELD:	2 dozen

1 egg white, room temperature
½ cup honey
⅛ teaspoon sea salt
1 tablespoon whole-wheat flour, unsifted
½ teaspoon vanilla
¼ teaspoon almond extract
1 cup almonds or pecans, finely ground
1 cup shredded coconut, unsweetened

1. Preheat oven to 350°F.

2. In a medium-sized bowl, mix together egg white, honey, salt, flour, and extracts.

3. Add almonds and coconut. Mix until batter is blended.

4. Drop batter by teaspoons on an oiled cookie sheet.

5. Bake 10–15 minutes or until cookies are lightly browned on the edges and soft on top.

6. Remove cookies from cookie sheet while they are still warm and cool on a wire rack.

Peanut Butter Cookies

Crunchy peanut butter makes a crunchier cookie.

PREPARATION TIME:	20 minutes
BAKING TIME:	10–12 minutes
COOLING TIME:	10 minutes
YIELD:	3 dozen

1 cup (2 sticks) butter or soy margarine, melted
1 cup honey
½ cup molasses
1 teaspoon vanilla
½ cup natural smooth peanut butter
1 cup whole-wheat pastry flour, unsifted
1½ cups unbleached flour, unsifted
¼ teaspoon baking powder
½ teaspoon sea salt

1. Preheat oven to 350°F.

2. Beat butter, honey, molasses, and vanilla until smooth.

3. Add peanut butter, flours, baking powder, and salt. Mix thoroughly.

4. Drop batter by half teaspoons onto an oiled cookie sheet.

5. Bake for 10–12 minutes or until cookies are brown around edges.

6. Remove the cookies with a spatula and cool on a rack.

Thumb-Print Cookies

A colorful addition to the dessert tray.

PREPARATION TIME:	15 minutes
BAKING TIME:	8–11 minutes
COOLING TIME:	10 minutes
YIELD:	2 dozen

$\frac{1}{2}$ *cup (1 stick) butter or soy margarine*
2 tablespoons honey
2 tablespoons molasses
$\frac{1}{2}$ *teaspoon vanilla*
1 large egg yolk, room temperature
$1\frac{1}{4}$ *cups unbleached flour, sifted*
$\frac{1}{2}$ *cup pecans, ground*

1. Preheat oven to 375°F.

2. Cream butter, honey, and molasses.

3. Add vanilla and egg yolk. Mix well.

4. Gradually add flour and ground pecans and mix.

5. Roll into 1-inch balls and place on an oiled cookie sheet 1 inch apart.

6. Press thumb into center of each cookie.

7. Bake for 8–11 minutes.

8. Remove from oven and cool cookies on a rack.

9. Fill thumb print with fruit spread, Carob Cream Frosting (see page 138), Butter Cream Frosting (see page 135), or puréed dates mixed with honey.

Spice Cookies

Molasses and spice and everything nice!

PREPARATION TIME:	20 minutes
BAKING TIME:	12–15 minutes
COOLING TIME:	10 minutes
YIELD:	3 dozen

1 cup (2 sticks) butter or soy margarine
1 cup molasses
¼ teaspoon sea salt
¼ teaspoon baking powder
¼ teaspoon nutmeg
¼ teaspoon cinnamon
½ teaspoon ginger
1 cup whole-wheat pastry flour, unsifted
1½ cups unbleached flour, unsifted

1. Preheat oven to 350°F.

2. Beat butter and molasses until creamy.

3. Add the remaining ingredients and beat until smooth.

4. Drop by teaspoons onto an oiled cookie sheet.

5. Bake 12–15 minutes or until cookies are brown around the edges.

6. Remove cookies with a spatula and cool on a rack.

Butter Nut Cookies

A good basic recipe—and a variation—for your cookie jar.

PREPARATION TIME:	20 minutes
BAKING TIME:	12–15 minutes
COOLING TIME:	10 minutes
YIELD:	2½ dozen

1 cup (2 sticks) butter or soy margarine, melted
¾ cup honey
¼ cup pure maple syrup
1 teaspoon vanilla
1 teaspoon almond extract
1½ cups unbleached flour, unsifted
1 cup whole-wheat pastry flour, unsifted
¼ teaspoon baking powder
½ teaspoon sea salt
1 cup nuts, finely chopped

1. Preheat oven to 350°F.

2. Beat butter, honey, syrup, and extracts in a large bowl. Set aside.

3. In a medium-sized bowl, combine remaining ingredients. Mix well.

4. Gradually combine dry mixture with liquid mixture and beat until smooth.

5. Drop batter by teaspoons onto an oiled cookie sheet.

6. Bake 12–15 minutes or until cookies are brown around the edges.

7. Remove cookies from oven and cool on a rack.

Variation

Carob Chip Cookies

Follow the recipe for regular Butter Nut Cookies except eliminate the almond extract and replace with 1 teaspoon molasses. In step 3, add 1 cup of unsweetened carob chips to the batter.

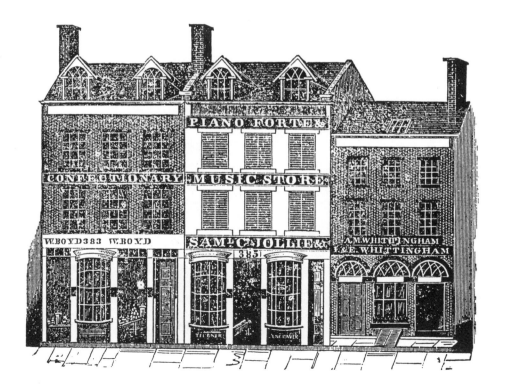

Oatmeal Cookies

A cookie in search of a glass of milk

PREPARATION TIME: 20 minutes
BAKING TIME: 8–12 minutes
COOLING TIME: 10 minutes
YIELD: $2\frac{1}{2}$ dozen

$\frac{1}{2}$ *cup (1 stick) butter or soy margarine*
$\frac{1}{2}$ *cup molasses*
$\frac{1}{4}$ *cup honey*
1 teaspoon vanilla
1 large egg, room temperature
$\frac{1}{2}$ *cup whole-wheat pastry flour, unsifted*
$\frac{1}{2}$ *cup unbleached flour, unsifted*
$\frac{1}{4}$ *teaspoon baking powder*
$\frac{1}{4}$ *teaspoon salt*
2 cups rolled oats
$\frac{1}{2}$ *cup pecans, chopped*

1. Preheat oven to 350°F.

2. In a large bowl, cream together butter, molasses, honey, vanilla, and egg.

3. Combine flours, baking powder, salt, oats, and pecans. Mix well.

4. Drop batter by teaspoons onto an oiled cookie sheet.

5. Bake 8–12 minutes or until cookies are golden brown around the edges and slightly soft in the center.

Pies and Pastries

The rich aroma of home-baked goodness
is a comforting reminder
of the simple pleasures of life.
Experience this fine array of old-fashioned
American pies and pastries.
They're just a page away.

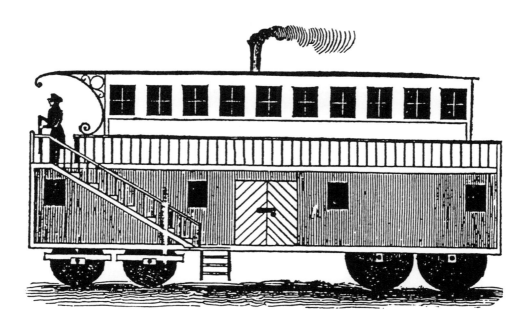

Hints

~ These recipes call for unsifted flour. When using commercially presifted flour, pack the flour tightly in the measuring cup by tapping the bottom of the cup on a hard surface.

~ To bake pie shells, select glass pie plates or dull metal pans. Shiny metal or aluminum pans will not brown the crust sufficiently, especially on the sides.

~ Pastry balls are much easier to roll out if the dough has been chilled for 30 minutes.

~ If you like to roll dough between sheets of wax paper, dampen the table surface before putting down the bottom sheet of paper. This will keep the paper from slipping.

~ For easy fluting, use scissors to cut the pastry $\frac{1}{2}$ inch beyond the edge of the pie plate. Fold the extra $\frac{1}{2}$ inch of pastry back in toward the center of the crust to make a thicker edge. After building up the edge, flute.

~ Fluting may be done with the floured tines of a fork, fingers, the bowl of a spoon, or the triangular end of a soft-drink-can opener.

~ Baked crusts can be removed from their plates after cooling. These "free-standing" crusts can be carefully stacked, wrapped, and frozen for quick use later.

~ Attractive double-crust pies can be achieved by brushing the top with milk, water, butter, or beaten egg yolk before baking.

~ Before baking fruit pies, place the pie plate on a cookie sheet to catch messy spills.

~ When baking custard pies, place the empty pie shell on the oven rack and then add the filling. This will prevent the filling's spilling over during baking.

~ Any of the pudding recipes on pages 107–113 can be used as a pie filling. The pudding must be chilled for 4–6 hours before the pie can be cut.

~ Create heavenly chiffon pies by filling a cool pie shell with mousse (see pages 159–166). Allow the pie to chill 3–4 hours before cutting.

Basic Pie Shell

The crust's the thing to catch a king.

PREPARATION TIME: 15 minutes
CHILLING TIME: 30 minutes
YIELD: 1 double-crust pie or 2 single-crust pies

2 cups unbleached flour, unsifted
½ teaspoon sea salt
1 recipe Smither Shortening (see next page)*
½ cup ice water

1. Mix flour and salt in a large bowl.

2. Cut in shortening with a knife or a pastry blender until the mixture resembles coarse meal.

3. Add ice water and stir with a fork until a ball can be formed. (If the mixture seems too crumbly and dry, add more ice water, 1 teaspoon at a time.)

4. Divide the ball in half. For ease in handling, chill the balls 30 minutes before rolling them out with a floured rolling pin.

5. Flatten the dough ball with your hands and roll it out on a well-floured surface. Work the rolling pin from the center to the edges until the dough is about 6 inches in diameter.

6. Turn the dough over, lightly flour the surface, and roll out again until a circle about 12 inches in diameter is formed.

7. Fold the dough circle in half and *ease it loosely* into a 9-inch pie plate. Unfold. (Do not stretch the dough. Stretching can cause the dough to buckle during baking.)

8. Trim and flute the edges.

9. Before baking an empty shell, prick the sides and bottom all over with a fork and preheat oven to 450°F.

10. Bake the shell at 450°F for 12–15 minutes or until it is golden brown. (Watch carefully during baking. If the crust puffs up, use the tines of a fork to push the dough in place.)

11. Cool shell completely before filling.

---

*You may substitute 10 tablespoons of chilled soy margarine or butter, but the crust will not be as flaky.

Smither Shortening

Here's the secret to flaky, tender pie crust.

PREPARATION TIME:	5 minutes
FREEZING TIME:	1 hour
YIELD:	10 tablespoons

6 tablespoons butter or soy margarine, melted
4 tablespoons vegetable oil

1. Combine melted butter and oil in a small cup or bowl.

2. Freeze mixture for 1 hour or until a solid has formed.

3. Use as you would shortening to make pie crust.

Whole-Wheat Pie Shell

Whole-wheat flour gives this crust a nutty flavor.

PREPARATION TIME:	15 minutes
CHILLING TIME:	30 minutes
YIELD:	1 nine-inch pie shell

⅔ cup unbleached flour
⅓ cup whole-wheat pastry flour
¼ teaspoon sea salt
½ recipe Smither Shortening (see page 66)*
¼ cup ice water

1. Mix flours and salt in a large bowl.

2. Cut in Smither Shortening with a knife or pastry blender until the dough resembles coarse meal.

3. Add ice water and stir until a ball can be formed. If the mixture seems too crumbly and dry, add more ice water, 1 teaspoon at a time. For ease in handling, chill the dough for 30 minutes before rolling it out with a floured rolling pin.

4. Flatten the dough ball with your hands and roll it out on a well-floured surface. Work the rolling pin from the center to the edges until the dough is about 6 inches in diameter.

5. Turn dough over once, lightly flour, and roll out again until a circle about 12 inches in diameter is formed.

6. Fold the dough circle in half and *ease it loosely* into a 9-inch pie plate. Unfold. (Do not stretch the dough. Stretching can cause the dough to buckle during baking.)

7. Trim and flute the edges.

8. Before baking an empty shell, prick the sides and bottom all over with a fork.

9. Bake shell at 450°F for 12–15 minutes or until it is golden brown. (Watch carefully during baking. If the crust puffs up, use the tines of a fork to push the dough in place.)

10. Cool shell completely before filling.

---

*You may substitute 5 tablespoons of chilled soy margarine or butter, but the crust will not be as flaky.

Quick Whole-Wheat Pie Shell

*For pies that do not need a top crust,
this hearty-tasting pastry can be pressed into shape
in a matter of minutes.*

PREPARATION TIME: 10 minutes
BAKING TIME: 12–15 minutes
YIELD: 1 nine-inch pie shell

1 cup + 2 tablespoons whole-wheat pastry flour, unsifted
¼ teaspoon sea salt
6 tablespoons oil
3 tablespoons cold water

1. In a medium-sized bowl, combine flour, salt, oil, and water.

2. Stir ingredients until a dough is formed that will hold together when it is pressed.

3. Transfer dough to a 9-inch pie plate. Using your hands, fingers, and the back of a spoon, press the dough evenly around the bottom and sides of the plate.

4. Flute the edges of the dough.

5. Before baking the empty shell, prick the sides and bottom all over with a fork.

6. Bake the shell at 450°F for 12–15 minutes or until it is light brown.

7. Cool shell completely before filling.

Crumb Shell

Perfect crust for chiffon pies, cream pies, and cheesecake.

PREPARATION TIME: 10 minutes
BAKING TIME: 10 minutes
YIELD: 1 nine-inch crumb shell

1¼ *cups crushed cookies or Graham Crackers (see page 52)*
¼ *cup (½ stick) butter or soy margarine, melted*
1 *teaspoon honey**

1. Break cookies or crackers into small pieces and place them in a paper or plastic bag. Use a rolling pin to hammer and roll until crumbs are finely crushed. (The crumbs can also be processed in a blender or food processor.)

2. Combine melted butter, honey, and 1¼ cups crumbs in a medium-sized bowl. Mix ingredients with your hands to evenly coat.

3. Press crumbs onto the sides and bottom of a pie plate until a firm, thin crust is formed. (To avoid a thick layer's forming in the corners, use the back of a spoon to press the crumbs.)

4. For prebaked crust, bake for 10 minutes at 375°F. Watch carefully to avoid overbaking.

5. Cool crust on a wire rack before filling.

---

*Do not use honey when preparing a crust that will be filled before baking. For recipes that request unbaked pie crust, eliminate the honey and refrigerate the crust at least 30 minutes before using.

Cinnamon Rolls

Our son begs for this breakfast treat.
These rolls are also great with fruit as a light dessert.

PREPARATION TIME: 25 minutes
BAKING TIME: 12 minutes
YIELD: 1 dozen rolls

Filling
¼ cup (½ stick) butter or soy margarine
⅓ cup honey
¼ teaspoon vanilla
2 teaspoons cinnamon

Batter
1 cup whole-wheat pastry flour, unsifted
1 cup unbleached flour, unsifted
1 teaspoon baking powder
½ teaspoon sea salt
½ cup milk, soy milk, or water
1 large egg, beaten

1. Preheat oven to 325°F.

2. In a medium-sized bowl, cream butter, honey, and vanilla to make the filling. Set aside.

3. Sift flours, baking powder, and salt into a large bowl.

4. Add milk and beaten egg. Stir vigorously until the dough can be formed into a ball with your hands. Dough will be sticky.

5. Turn onto a well-floured surface and knead slightly. Do not overwork.

6. Roll and trim dough into a rectangle about 12 inches x 10 inches.

7. Spread filling evenly over the entire surface with a spatula. Sprinkle with cinnamon.

8. Roll tightly along the width. Seal the edge by pressing it into the roll.

9. Cut into 12 one-inch slices. Place each slice in a well-oiled muffin pan.

10. Bake 10–12 minutes.

11. Let rolls cool 5 minutes before removing from pan.

12. If desired, sprinkle tops with crushed nuts and Maple Sugar (see page 132).

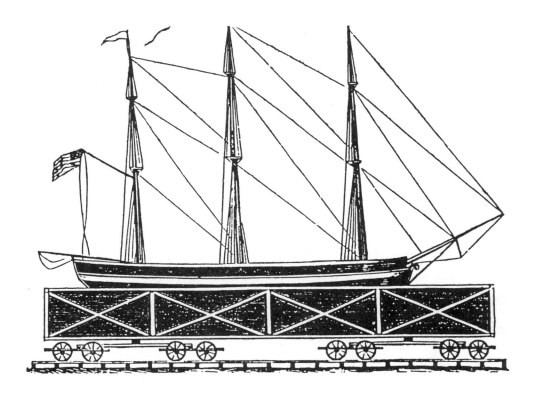

Cream Puffs

Much easier than they look.

PREPARATION TIME:	25 minutes
BAKING TIME:	30 minutes
COOLING TIME:	20 minutes
YIELD:	8–10 servings

½ cup (1 stick) butter or soy margarine
1 cup water
⅛ teaspoon sea salt
½ cup whole-wheat pastry flour, unsifted
½ cup unbleached flour, unsifted
4 large eggs

1. Preheat oven to 400°F.

2. In a medium-sized saucepan, combine butter, water, and salt. Bring to a boil.

3. Add flours all at once. Stir vigorously.

4. Continue to cook and stir until mixture pulls away from sides of pan, forming a ball.

5. Remove pan from heat. Cool about 10 minutes.

6. Add eggs one at a time, beating with a wooden spoon after each addition until batter is smooth.

7. Drop batter by heaping tablespoons 3 inches apart on oiled cookie sheet.

8. Bake 30 minutes or until puffs are golden brown.

9. Cool puffs on a wire rack.

10. Split puffs. Remove any soft or wet dough from the inside before filling.

11. Fill with pudding, whipped cream, ice cream, or fruit.

12. Replace top and drizzle with Carob Syrup (see page 144).

Variation

Eclairs

Follow the directions for Cream Puffs but spread and shape the dough lengthwise on the baking sheet.

Apple Pie

A naturally sweet slice of Americana.

PREPARATION TIME: 20 minutes
BAKING TIME: 50 minutes
COOLING TIME: 1 hour or until room temperature
YIELD: 9-inch pie, 8 servings

¼ cup unbleached flour, unsifted
⅛ teaspoon sea salt
1 teaspoon cinnamon
¼ teaspoon nutmeg
1 cup honey
1 teaspoon lemon juice
2 tablespoons butter or soy margarine
4 cups thinly sliced apples or one 20-ounce
can unsweetened apples, drained
pastry for a 9-inch double-crust pie

1. Preheat oven to 375°F.

2. Combine flour, salt, cinnamon, nutmeg, honey, and lemon juice in a medium-sized pan. Cook on medium heat and stir until mixture is smooth and slightly thick.

3. Stir in butter.

4. Spread apples in an unbaked pie shell.

5. Pour mixture evenly over top of apples.

6. Vent top crust by poking it with a fork or cutting designs in it, and adjust over filling.

7. Seal and flute the edges.

8. Cover edges with foil and bake 25 minutes.

9. Remove foil and bake an additional 25 minutes.

10. Cool pie on a wire rack.

Partially-Baked Pie Shell

Use these shells and say "good-bye" to soggy crusts on custard pies.

PREPARATION TIME: 10 minutes
BAKING TIME: 15 minutes
YIELD: 1 nine-inch partially-baked pie shell

1 unbaked Basic or Whole-Wheat Pie Shell (see pages 65 and 67)

1. Preheat oven to 425°F.

2. Cut a piece of aluminum foil slightly larger than the pie plate.

3. Place the foil shiny-side down over the unbaked pastry shell.

4. Gently mold the foil to the shape of the shell.

5. Cover the bottom of the foil with beans, rice, or pie weights.

6. Bake 10–12 minutes.

7. Remove foil and weights and bake 3–5 minutes.

Cherry Pie

Rediscover this American treasure.

PREPARATION TIME:	20 minutes
BAKING TIME:	50 minutes
COOLING TIME:	1 hour or until room temperature
YIELD:	9-inch pie, 8 servings

2 cups canned sour pitted cherries (one 16-ounce can)
⅓ cup unbleached flour, unsifted
¼ teaspoon sea salt
1¼ cups honey
1 tablespoon butter or soy margarine
¼ teaspoon almond extract
pastry for a 9-inch double-crust pie

1. Preheat oven to 375°F.

2. Drain juice from canned cherries and reserve ½ cup. Set cherries aside.

3. In a medium-sized pan, blend cherry juice, flour, salt, and honey. Cook over medium heat and stir until mixture is smooth and slightly thick.

4. Add butter, almond extract, and cherries. Mix and pour into unbaked pie shell.

5. Vent top crust by poking it with a fork or cutting designs in it, and adjust crust over filling.

6. Seal and flute the edges.

7. Cover edges with foil and bake 25 minutes.

8. Remove foil cover and bake an additional 25 minutes.

9. Cool pie on a wire rack.

Crumb Topped Fruit Pies

An easy alternative to the double-crust pie.

PREPARATION TIME: 5 minutes
BAKING TIME: 50 minutes
YIELD: 9-inch pie, 8 servings

fruit-pie filling
unbaked 9-inch pie shell
1/3 cup whole-wheat pastry flour, unsifted
3 tablespoons butter or soy margarine
1 1/2 tablespoons molasses or maple syrup

1. Preheat oven to 375°F.

2. Pour fruit-pie filling into unbaked pie shell.

3. Measure flour into a medium-sized bowl.

4. Cut in butter until mixture resembles coarse meal.

5. Sprinkle mixture evenly over fruit filling.

6. Drizzle molasses or maple syrup over the top.

7. Cover edges with foil and bake 25 minutes.

8. Remove foil cover and bake an additional 25 minutes.

Peach Pie

Always a favorite

PREPARATION TIME:	20 minutes
BAKING TIME:	50 minutes
COOLING TIME:	1 hour or until room temperature
YIELD:	9-inch pie, 8 servings

⅓ cup unbleached flour, unsifted
⅛ teaspoon sea salt
¼ teaspoon nutmeg
⅛ teaspoon cinnamon
1 teaspoon lemon juice
2 tablespoons butter or soy margarine
1 cup honey
3 cups fresh, sliced peaches or
2 cups canned, drained, unsweetened peaches
pastry for a 9-inch double-crust pie

1. Preheat oven to 375°F.

2. Combine flour, salt, nutmeg, cinnamon, lemon juice, butter, and honey in a medium-sized pan. Cook on medium heat and stir until mixture is smooth and slightly thick.

3. Spread sliced peaches in unbaked pie shell and pour mixture evenly over the top.

4. Vent top crust by poking it with a fork or cutting designs in it, and adjust crust over filling.

5. Seal and flute the edges.

6. Cover edges with foil and bake 25 minutes.

7. Remove foil cover and bake an additional 25 minutes.

8. Cool pie on a wire rack.

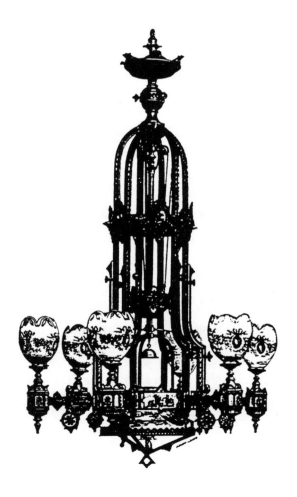

Pineapple Pie

A dessert that shouldn't be overlooked.

PREPARATION TIME:	20 minutes
BAKING TIME:	50 minutes
COOLING TIME:	1 hour or until room temperature
YIELD:	9-inch double-crust pie, 8 servings

¼ cup unbleached flour, unsifted
⅛ teaspoon sea salt
1 cup honey
2 tablespoons butter or soy margarine
1 teaspoon lemon juice
½ teaspoon vanilla
20-ounce can unsweetened, crushed pineapple, drained
pastry for a 9-inch double-crust pie

1. Preheat oven to 375°F.

2. Combine flour, salt, honey, butter, lemon juice, and vanilla in a medium-sized pan. Cook on medium heat and stir until mixture is smooth and slightly thick.

3. Add pineapple and mix until blended.

4. Pour mixture into unbaked pie shell.

5. Vent crust by poking it with a fork or cutting designs in it, and adjust crust over filling.

6. Seal and flute the edges.

7. Cover edges with foil and bake 25 minutes.

8. Remove foil cover and bake an additional 25 minutes.

9. Cool pie on a wire rack.

Mincemeatless Pie

*Measures up to the real thing in taste, texture,
and appearance.*

PREPARATION TIME:	30 minutes
BAKING TIME:	50 minutes
COOLING TIME:	1 hour or until room temperature
YIELD:	9-inch pie, 8 servings

*4 medium-sized apples, coarsely ground
1 coarsely ground seeded orange, peel included
1 cup dark raisins, coarsely ground
1 cup pecans, ground
1 teaspoon cinnamon
$\frac{1}{2}$ teaspoon nutmeg
$\frac{1}{2}$ teaspoon ground cloves
$\frac{1}{8}$ teaspoon sea salt
1 cup honey
$\frac{1}{2}$ tablespoon lemon juice
2 tablespoons melted butter or soy margarine
2 tablespoons whole-wheat flour, unsifted
pastry for a 9-inch double-crust pie*

1. Preheat oven to 375°F.

2. In a large bowl, mix ground fruit, pecans, and spices with remaining ingredients, except the pastry. (Mixture may be used immediately or refrigerated in a closed container for up to a week to heighten flavor.)

3. Spread mixture evenly in an unbaked pie shell.

4 Vent top crust by poking it with a fork or cutting designs in it, and adjust crust over filling.

5. Seal and flute the edges.

6. Cover edges with foil and bake 25 minutes.

7. Remove foil and bake an additional 25 minutes.

8. Cool pie on a wire rack.

Cobbler I

It's quick and easy!
The top becomes the bottom and the bottom becomes the top!
Serve it while it's hot.

PREPARATION TIME:	20 minutes
BAKING TIME:	40 minutes
YIELD:	12 half-cup servings

Filling
14- to 20-ounce can unsweetened fruit
(apple, cherry, peach, pineapple, blueberry, blackberry, or fruit cocktail)
1 cup honey
1 teaspoon lemon juice
½ teaspoon cinnamon (omit for cherry or pineapple filling)

Batter
¾ cup whole-wheat pastry flour, unsifted
¾ cup unbleached flour, unsifted
¼ teaspoon sea salt
½ teaspoon baking powder
2 large eggs, room temperature
½ cup (1 stick) butter or soy margarine, melted
¾ cup milk or soy milk, room temperature
½ cup reserved juice or water, room temperature

1. Preheat oven to 375°F.

2. Drain fruit, reserving $\frac{1}{2}$ cup juice, if desired, for batter.

3. In a medium-sized bowl, combine fruit, honey, lemon juice, and cinnamon.

4. In another bowl, combine flours, salt, baking powder. Stir with wooden spoon to mix well.

5. Add eggs and melted butter.

6. Gradually add milk while beating with an electric mixer.

7. When batter is free of lumps, add juice or water and beat until smooth.

8. Spread batter evenly into a well-oiled 2-quart or 11-inch x 7-inch baking dish.

9. Spread fruit filling evenly over top of batter.

10. Bake for 40 minutes or until a toothpick inserted in the middle comes out clean.

11. Serve warm, plain or with cream.

Cobbler II

Old-fashioned country goodness!

PREPARATION TIME: 30 minutes
BAKING TIME: 45 minutes
YIELD: 12 half-cup servings

14- to 20-ounce can unsweetened fruit
(apple, cherry, peach, pineapple, blueberry, blackberry, or fruit cocktail)
¼ cup unbleached flour
⅛ teaspoon sea salt
½ teaspoon cinnamon (omit for cherry or pineapple filling)
1 teaspoon lemon juice
1 cup honey
2 tablespoons butter or soy margarine
½ cup reserved fruit juice or water
1 whole-wheat pie crust (see page 67)

1. Preheat oven to 375°F.

2. Drain fruit, reserving ½ cup of juice. Set aside.

3. In a medium-sized pan, combine flour, salt, cinnamon, lemon juice, butter or margarine, and fruit juice or water.

4. Cook over medium heat, stirring constantly only until butter is melted and mixture is smooth. Do not allow the mixture to thicken.

5. Add fruit, stir, and pour into a well-oiled 2-quart or 11-inch x 7-inch baking dish. Set aside.

6. Roll out whole-wheat pie crust until it is $\frac{1}{8}$-inch thick. Cut into strips and make a lattice pattern over the fruit filling, or cut vent holes into the crust, trim the crust to the size of the baking dish, and cover the fruit filling.

7. Bake at 375°F for 40–45 minutes or until crust is golden brown.

8. Serve warm, plain or with cream.

Variation

Fresh Fruit Cobbler

Substitute 3 cups sliced or chopped fresh fruit for canned fruit and $\frac{1}{2}$ cup water for reserved fruit juice.

Pecan Pie

A real luxury, the sweetest of all pies.

PREPARATION TIME:	15 minutes
BAKING TIME:	45 minutes
COOLING TIME:	1½ hours or until room temperature
YIELD:	9-inch pie, 8 servings

1 cup pecan halves or chopped pecans
1 partially-baked 9-inch pie shell (see page 76)
2 tablespoons arrowroot or cornstarch
½ cup milk, cream, or soy milk
¼ cup (½ stick) butter or soy margarine, melted
1 cup honey
⅓ cup unsulphured molasses
⅛ teaspoon sea salt
2 large egg yolks + 2 large whole eggs

1. Bring all ingredients to room temperature.

2. Preheat oven to 350°F.

3. Spread pecans evenly on the bottom of a partially baked 9-inch pie shell. Set aside.

4. In a small cup or bowl, combine arrowroot or cornstarch and milk. Stir until arrowroot is completely dissolved. Set aside.

5. In a medium-sized bowl, combine butter, honey, molasses, salt, and arrowroot mixture. Beat until ingredients are thoroughly mixed.

6. Add yolks and eggs and beat 5 seconds with mixer on high speed.

7. Remove any excess foam and pour mixture into pie shell.

8. Cover the edge of the pie shell with a ring of foil and bake for 45 minutes.

9. Cool pie for $1\frac{1}{2}$ hours or until room temperature.

Variations

Pecan Pie II

Follow directions for Pecan Pie but do not add pecans in step 3. Follow the remaining directions except bake the pie for only 35 minutes. Let the pie cool for 1 hour before removing the carmalized skin on the pie's surface with a fork. Spread pecans on top of the pie at random or in a pattern, and press them into the pie's surface with a fork.

Oatmeal Pie

Follow the directions for Pecan Pie except substitute $\frac{3}{4}$ cup uncooked rolled oats and $\frac{1}{4}$ cup unsweetened coconut for pecans. Bake for 45 minutes as indicated.

Maple Walnut Pie

Follow the directions for Pecan Pie except decrease milk to $\frac{1}{4}$ cup and substitute walnuts for pecans. Eliminate honey and molasses and substitute $1\frac{1}{3}$ cups pure maple syrup. Bake for 35 minutes.

Pumpkin Pie

*Even though we associate this pie with the holidays,
don't wait to try it or its tasty variations.*

PREPARATION TIME:	15 minutes
BAKING TIME:	50 minutes
COOLING TIME:	1 hour or until room temperature
YIELD:	9-inch pie, 8 servings

*8 ounces cream cheese, softened, or
½ cup cream, milk, or soy milk, room temperature
1 cup honey
2 tablespoons molasses
16-ounce can unsweetened pumpkin or
2 cups fresh pumpkin purée
1 teaspoon cinnamon
½ teaspoon nutmeg
¼ teaspoon sea salt
2 large eggs, room temperature
1 partially baked 9-inch pie shell (see page 76)*

1. Preheat oven to 375°F.

2. Beat together cream cheese (or cream or milk), honey, and molasses until blended.

3. Add pumpkin, cinnamon, nutmeg, and salt.

4. Add eggs and beat until smooth.

5. Pour into partially baked 9-inch pie shell.

6. Cover the edge of the shell with a ring of foil.

7. Bake 50 minutes.

8. Remove pie from oven and cool on a rack to room temperature.

Variations

Sweet Potato Pie

Peel and dice 3 large sweet potatoes. Cook until tender in just enough water to cover. Drain, mash, and reserve 2 cups for pie filling. Follow the directions for Pumpkin Pie.

Butternut Squash Pie

Peel and slice one medium-sized squash. Cook until tender in just enough water to cover. Drain, mash, and reserve 2 cups for pie filling. Follow the directions for Pumpkin Pie.

Chess Pie

Modest cooks claimed, "It's jest pie."
Southern dialect turned this favorite into "Chess Pie."

PREPARATION TIME:	20 minutes
BAKING TIME:	35 minutes
COOLING TIME:	1 hour or until room temperature
YIELD:	9-inch pie, 8 servings

2 tablespoons arrowroot or cornstarch
½ cup milk, cream, or soy milk
¼ cup (½ stick) butter or soy margarine, melted
1 cup honey
2 tablespoons lemon or lime juice
⅛ teaspoon sea salt
1 teaspoon vanilla
2 large egg yolks + 2 large whole eggs, beaten
1 partially baked 9-inch pie shell (see page 76)

1. Bring all ingredients to room temperature.

2. Preheat oven to 350°F.

3. In a small cup or bowl, combine arrowroot and milk. Stir until arrowroot is completely dissolved. Set aside.

4. In a medium-sized bowl, combine butter, honey, lemon juice, salt, vanilla, and arrowroot mixture. Beat until ingredients are thoroughly mixed.

5. Add yolks and eggs and beat 5 seconds with mixer on high speed.

6. Remove any excess foam and pour the mixture into a partially baked 9-inch pie shell.

7. Bake for 35 minutes. (Overbaking will cause the custard to be watery.)

8. Cool pie for 1 hour or until room temperature.

Variation

Coconut Chess Pie

Follow the directions for Chess Pie. Add ½ cup unsweetened coconut just before pouring the filling into the shell.

Custard Pie

*The person who coined the phrase, "It's easy as pie,"
must have been thinking about the ease with which
this simple delicacy goes together.*

PREPARATION TIME:	20 minutes
BAKING TIME:	40 minutes
COOLING TIME:	1 hour or until room temperature
YIELD:	9-inch pie, 8 servings

*9-inch pie shell made with unbleached
flour (see page 65), chilled**
1 tablespoon butter, softened**
½ cup honey
¼ teaspoon sea salt
1 teaspoon vanilla
2 cups milk, cream, or soy milk
6 large egg yolks (½ cup)
dash of nutmeg

1. With your fingertips, spread butter evenly on the bottom and sides of chilled pie shell to form a smooth protective coating.

2. Place prepared shell in the refrigerator while filling is being made. Bring all other ingredients to room temperature.

3. Preheat oven to 450°F.

4. In a medium-sized bowl, combine honey, salt, vanilla, and milk. Beat until ingredients are well mixed.

5. Add egg yolks and beat for 5 seconds with mixer at high speed.

6. Remove any excess foam and pour mixture into pie shell.

7. Bake pie for 10 minutes at 450°F and then 30 minutes at 350°F.

8. Remove pie from oven, sprinkle with nutmeg, and cool for 1 hour or until room temperature.

---

*Whole-Wheat Pie Shells must be partially baked. To use these shells, eliminate step 2. Place a ring of foil around the edge of the pie shell before baking it.

**Margarine will not work with this recipe. The coating of butter gives the crust time to brown before the filling can seep into the dough.

Lemon Meringue Pie

A tangy slice of sunshine with which to finish any meal.

PREPARATION TIME:	25 minutes
BAKING TIME:	15 minutes
CHILLING TIME:	4–6 hours
YIELD:	9-inch pie, 8 servings

⅓ cup arrowroot or cornstarch
2 cups orange juice
¾ cup honey
¼ cup lemon juice
⅛ teaspoon sea salt
4 large egg yolks, beaten
1 prebaked 9-inch pie shell (see pages 65–69)
or crumb shell (see page 70)
1 tablespoon butter or soy margarine
3–4 egg whites

1. Combine arrowroot and ½ cup of orange juice in a large cup. Stir to dissolve arrowroot, and then set aside.

2. In a medium-sized pan, cook honey, lemon juice, salt and remaining orange juice on medium heat.

3. When the mixture begins to steam, add arrowroot mixture. Stir constantly until mixture is smooth.

4. Gradually stir several tablespoons of hot mixture into beaten egg yolks.

5. Add egg yolk mixture to the hot mixture in the pan.

6. Continue cooking until mixture is smooth and well blended. *Do not boil.* (Remove any cooked egg particles.)

7. Remove from heat and add butter.

8. Allow mixture to cool slightly and pour it into pie shell.

9. Beat egg whites until soft peaks form (meringue).

10. Apply meringue to the top of the filling while it is still warm. Seal by smoothing meringue to the edges of the crust.

11. Bake at 350°F for 12–15 minutes or until meringue is golden brown.

12. Cool pie away from drafts.

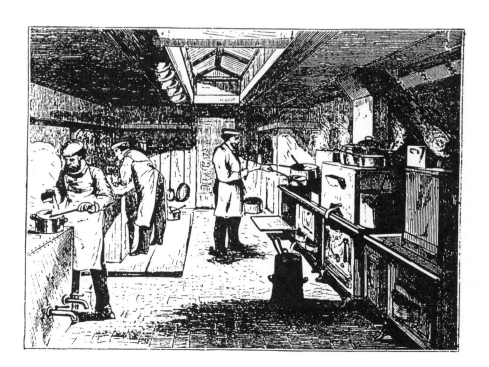

Carob Chiffon Pie

A perfect introduction to the goodness of carob.

PREPARATION TIME:	30 minutes
CHILLING TIME:	3–4 hours
YIELD:	9-inch pie, 8 servings

1 tablespoon (1 envelope) unflavored gelatin
¼ cup water
¾ cup honey
¼ cup carob powder, sifted
¼ teaspoon sea salt
¾ cup milk
3 egg yolks, slightly beaten
3 egg whites, chilled
1 cup heavy cream, whipped
1 prebaked 9-inch pie shell (see pages 65–69)
or crumb shell (see page 70)

1. Separate eggs and chill whites till you are ready to use them (step 11).

2. Mix gelatin and water in a small bowl.

3. Place the small bowl in a large bowl of hot water until gelatin is dissolved and mixture is clear. Set aside.

4. Combine honey, carob powder, and salt in a small pan and mix until a thick paste forms.

5. Stir in milk and cook mixture over medium heat until it is hot.

6. Gradually stir several tablespoons of hot mixture into egg yolks.

7. Add the egg yolk mixture to remaining mixture in the pan.

8. Continue to cook mixture over medium heat, stirring constantly until it is smooth and slightly thick. (Remove any cooked egg particles.)

9. Remove mixture from heat.

10. Add gelatin, stirring until evenly mixed.

11. Transfer mixture to a large bowl and chill for 1 hour or until it is partially set.

12. Beat egg whites until they are stiff.

13. Fold beaten egg whites into chilled mixture then fold in whipped cream until mixture is smooth and well mixed.

14. Turn into cooled pie shell and refrigerate pie until it is firm.

Variations

To create other varieties of chiffon pie, fill a baked pie shell with any mousse (see pages 159–166). Chill the pie for 3–4 hours before cutting.

Molasses Crumb Pie (Shoo-Fly Pie)

Yes, you can make this Pennsylvania Dutch delight
without baking soda.

PREPARATION TIME:	20 minutes
BAKING TIME:	30 minutes
YIELD:	9-inch pie, 8 servings

Crumb Mixture
1 cup whole-wheat pastry flour, unsifted
½ teaspoon cinnamon
⅛ teaspoon nutmeg
⅛ teaspoon ginger
¼ teaspoon sea salt
½ cup (1 stick) butter or soy margarine

Liquid Mixture
½ cup molasses
¼ cup honey
⅓ cup boiling water
1 teaspoon baking powder
1 large egg yolk, well beaten

Pastry Shell
9-inch shell (see pages 65–69)

1. Preheat oven to 450°F.

2. Mix together flour, spices, and salt.

3. Cut in butter with pastry blender or two knives until mixture resembles coarse meal. Set aside.

4. Combine molasses, honey, boiling water, baking powder, and egg. Stir to mix.

5. In a 9-inch pastry shell, alternate layers of crumb mixture and liquid mixture, ending with crumbs. (Sprinkle nuts on top, if desired.)

6. Bake at 450°F for 10 minutes.

7. Reduce heat to 350°F and bake pie for an additional 20 minutes or until a toothpick inserted in the center comes out clean.

8. Serve plain as a breakfast pastry or topped with whipped cream as a dessert.

Fruit
Cream Cheese Pie

A dessert that is unique in itself, and the filling can be a frosting.

PREPARATION TIME: 25 minutes
CHILLING TIME: 1 hour
YIELD: 9-inch pie, 8 servings

1 teaspoon unflavored gelatin
2 tablespoons water
1 cup (½-pint carton) heavy cream
8 ounces cream cheese, room temperature
½ cup honey
2 cups fresh fruit or a 16-ounce can of fruit,
finely chopped and well drained
1 prebaked 9-inch pastry shell or
crumb crust (see pages 65–70)

1. Mix gelatin and water in a cup.

2. Place the cup in a bowl of hot water until gelatin is dissolved and mixture is clear. Set aside.

3. Whip cream in a medium-sized bowl until it is firm.

4. Add the dissolved gelatin and beat mixture for 30 seconds until blended.

5. Refrigerate for 15 minutes.

6. In a large bowl, combine cream cheese, honey, and fruit. Whip until mixture is smooth.

7. Add whipped cream to cream cheese mixture and blend.

8. Pour mixture into a prebaked pastry shell and refrigerate for 1 hour before serving.

Puddings

Whether cooked, baked, or steamed,
pudding spells s-u-c-c-e-s-s.
It's amazing that these time-tested desserts
made from the most basic of ingredients
can still receive a royal fanfare.

Hints

ೆ These recipes call for unsifted flour. When using commercially presifted flour, pack the flour tightly in the measuring cup by tapping the bottom of the cup on a hard surface.

ೆ To make a sauce from the cream pudding recipes, add milk or soy milk to the mixture and cook until desired consistency is formed.

ೆ To prevent a skin from forming on the surface of a pudding, cover the top with a layer of plastic wrap while the pudding is still warm and just before refrigerating.

ೆ Freeze those leftover egg whites in a container marked with amount or freeze them individually in ice trays for a storage life of about a year.

ೆ Any pudding on pages 107–113 can be used as a pie filling. Filling must be chilled 4–6 hours before pie is cut.

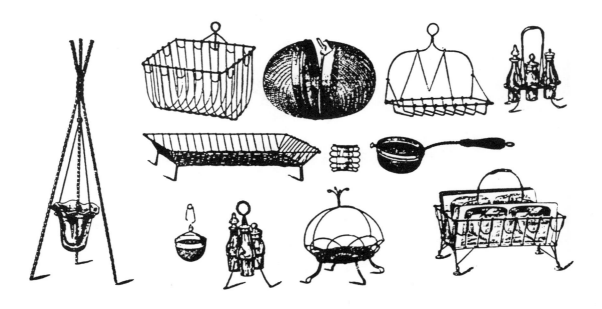

Vanilla Cream Pudding

Sweet, silky, and scrumptious.

PREPARATION TIME: 25 minutes
YIELD: 6 half-cup servings

¼ cup unbleached flour, unsifted
¼ teaspoon sea salt
½ cup honey
2 cups milk or soy milk
4 large egg yolks, beaten
2 tablespoons butter or soy margarine
2 teaspoons vanilla

1. Blend four, salt, and honey in a pan. Stir until a smooth, thick paste forms.

2. Add milk gradually, stirring until mixture is smooth.

3. Cook mixture over medium heat, stirring constantly until it is smooth and thick.

4. Gradually stir several tablespoons of hot mixture into yolks.

5. Add egg yolk mixture to remaining mixture in the pan.

6. Continue cooking until mixture is smooth and thick. *Do not boil.*

7. Remove mixture from heat (remove any cooked egg particles) and add butter and vanilla, stirring until blended.

8. Pour into pudding cups. Pudding may be eaten warm or chilled. Top with your favorite fresh fruit, drained canned fruit, or whipped cream.

Variations

Peanut Butter Cream Pudding

Follow Vanilla Cream Pudding recipe except add 1 tablespoon molasses and 2 tablespoons smooth unsalted peanut butter. Decrease vanilla to ½ teaspoon.

Banana Cream Pudding

Follow Vanilla Cream Pudding recipe except spread 3 medium bananas, sliced (2 cups) over bottom of pudding cups. Pour filling on top

Butterscotch Cream Pudding

Follow Vanilla Cream Pudding recipe except substitute 1 tablespoon molasses for vanilla

Coconut Cream Pudding

Follow Vanilla Cream Pudding recipe except add ½ cup unsweetened shredded or flaked coconut.

Lemon Pudding

A tangy and smooth confection that deserves its reputation.

PREPARATION TIME: 25 minutes
YIELD: 6 half-cup servings

⅓ *cup arrowroot or cornstarch*
¾ *cup honey*
¼ *cup lemon juice*
2 cups orange juice
4 large egg yolks, beaten
⅛ *teaspoon sea salt*
1 tablespoon butter or soy margarine

1. Combine arrowroot and ½ cup of orange juice in a large cup. Stir to dissolve arrowroot, and then set aside.

2. In a medium-sized pan, cook honey, lemon juice, and remaining orange juice on medium heat.

3. When the mixture begins to steam, add arrowroot mixture. Stir constantly until smooth

4. Gradually stir several tablespoons of hot mixture into egg yolks.

5. Add egg yolk mixture to the remaining mixture in the pan.

6. Continue cooking until mixture is smooth and well blended. *Do not boil.*

7. Remove from heat (remove any cooked egg particles) and add butter.

8. Allow mixture to cool slightly. Pour into pudding cups. Pudding may be eaten warm or chilled. If desired, top pudding with whipped cream.

Variations

Lemon Pineapple Pudding

Follow directions for Lemon Pudding except substitute pineapple juice for orange juice. If desired, add an 8-ounce can of unsweetened, crushed pineapple, drained.

Lemon Cream Pudding

Follow the directions for Lemon Pudding except substitute milk, or cream, or soy milk for orange juice.

Maple Cream Pudding

Extravagant but worth it!

PREPARATION TIME: 25 minutes
YIELD: 5 half-cup servings

¼ *cup unbleached flour, unsifted*
¼ *teaspoon sea salt*
¾ *cup pure maple syrup*
1¾ *cups milk or soy milk*
3 large egg yolks, beaten
2 tablespoons butter or soy margarine

1. Blend flour, salt, and syrup in a pan.

2. Stir until a smooth, thick paste forms.

3. Add milk gradually, stirring until mixture is smooth.

4. Cook mixture over medium heat, stirring constantly until it is smooth and thick.

5. Gradually stir several tablespoons of hot mixture into yolks.

6. Add egg yolk mixture to the remaining mixture in the pan.

7. Continue cooking until mixture is smooth and thick. *Do not boil.*

8. Remove mixture from heat (remove any cooked egg particles) and add butter, stirring until blended.

9. Pour into pudding cups. Pudding may be eaten warm or chilled. Top with whipped cream or meringue.

Variation

Maple Nut Pudding

Add ½ cup finely chopped nuts to Maple Cream Pudding recipe.

Carob Cream Pudding

Our teenager's favorite.

PREPARATION TIME: 25 minutes
YIELD: 6 half-cup servings

¼ *cup unbleached flour, unsifted*
⅛ *teaspoon sea salt*
2 tablespoons carob powder
⅔ *cup honey*
2 cups milk or soy milk
4 large egg yolks, beaten
2 tablespoons butter or soy margarine
2 teaspoons vanilla

1. Blend flour, salt, and carob powder in a pan.

2. Add honey and stir until a smooth, thick paste forms.

3. Add 1 cup of milk at a time, mixing thoroughly after each addition.

4. Cook mixture over medium heat, stirring constantly until it is smooth and thick.

5. Gradually stir several tablespoons of hot mixture into yolks.

6. Add egg yolk mixture to the remaining mixture in the pan.

7. Continue cooking until mixture is smooth and thick. *Do not boil.*

8. Remove mixture from heat (remove any cooked egg particles) and add butter and vanilla, stirring until blended.

9. Pour into pudding cups. Pudding may be eaten warm or chilled. Top with meringue or whipped cream and sprinkle with chopped nuts.

Custard

A creamy, smooth delicacy that melts in the mouth.

PREPARATION TIME:	20 minutes
BAKING TIME:	50 minutes
COOLING TIME:	1 hour
YIELD:	6 half-cup servings

6 large egg yolks (¹/₂ cup)
¹/₂ cup honey
1 teaspoon vanilla
¹/₄ teaspoon sea salt
2 cups milk, cream, or soy milk
dash of nutmeg

1. *Do not preheat the oven.* All ingredients should be at room temperature.

2. Beat egg yolks, honey, vanilla, salt, and milk together in a bowl until they are well blended but not foamy. (Skim off any foam that may form.)

3. Pour mixture into 6 custard cups or into 1-quart baking dish.

4. Place a large dish or pan on the middle rack of a cold oven. Set custard cups in the pan and fill pan with hot water until the water reaches half-way up the custard cups.

5. Bake at 350°F for 50 minutes.

6. Remove custard cups from oven, sprinkle tops of custard with nutmeg, and cool on a rack to room temperature before refrigerating.

Variation

Flan

Butter the bottom and sides of the custard cups before following the recipe for Custard. After the custard has cooled for 1 hour, run a sharp knife around the rim of each cup, shake to loosen, invert on a serving dish. Remove cup and top custard with maple syrup or sprinkle with Maple Brown Sugar (see page 132).

Indian Pudding

Our rendition of an early American treat.

PREPARATION TIME: 20 minutes
BAKING TIME: 90 minutes
YIELD: 8–10 servings

4 cups milk or soy milk
1 cup corn meal
½ teaspoon sea salt
½ teaspoon cinnamon
½ teaspoon nutmeg
¼ teaspoon ginger
½ cup honey
½ cup molasses
¼ cup (½ stick) butter or soy margarine
2 large eggs, beaten

1   Preheat oven to 325°F.

2.   On medium-high heat, cook milk in a large saucepan until it comes to a rolling boil.

3.   Slowly sprinkle corn meal into hot milk, whisking constantly to prevent lumps.

4.   Lower heat and continue stirring.

5.   When mixture begins to thicken, add salt, spices, honey, molasses, and butter.

6.   Cool mixture slightly before blending in eggs.

7.   Pour mixture into a buttered 2-quart baking dish.

8.   Bake for 90 minutes.

9.   Remove from oven. (The center of the pudding will become firmer as it cools.)

10.   Serve warm or cold with whipped cream or ice cream.

Bread Pudding

An economical use of leftover bread.
Freeze bits and pieces of bread until you have enough
for this traditional favorite.

PREPARATION TIME: 20 minutes
BAKING TIME: 40 minutes
YIELD: 6 half-cup servings

2 cups (4 slices) whole-wheat bread cubes ($\frac{1}{4}$–$\frac{1}{2}$ inch),
toasted and buttered
$\frac{1}{2}$ cup seedless raisins
$\frac{1}{3}$ cup honey
2 tablespoons molasses or maple syrup
1 teaspoon vanilla
$\frac{1}{4}$ teaspoon sea salt
$1\frac{1}{2}$ cups milk or soy milk
2 large eggs, beaten
$\frac{1}{2}$ teaspoon cinnamon

1. Preheat oven to 350°F.

2. Place bread cubes and raisins in the bottom of a 1-quart casserole. Set aside.

3. Combine sweeteners, vanilla, salt, and milk in a pan. Warm and mix thoroughly over low heat. *Do not boil.*

4. Gradually add eggs and mix.

5. Pour warm liquid over bread cubes and raisins.

6. Sprinkle with cinnamon.

7. Bake 35–40 minutes or until knife inserted in center comes out clean.

8. Serve warm or cool with cream or Lemon Sauce (see page 142) if desired.

Rice Pudding

Cook extra rice for dinner then turn the leftovers into this splendid pudding.

PREPARATION TIME:	15 minutes
BAKING TIME:	50 minutes
YIELD:	6 half-cup servings

3 large eggs
1½ cups milk or soy milk
⅓ cup honey
1 teaspoon vanilla
⅛ teaspoon sea salt
2 cups brown rice, cooked
nutmeg or cinnamon

1. Preheat oven to 325°F.

2. Combine eggs, milk, honey, vanilla, and salt in medium-sized bowl. Beat until foamy.

3. Add rice and pour into 1½-quart casserole.

4. Sprinkle with nutmeg or cinnamon.

5. Bake for 50 minutes.

6. Dot with butter.

7. Serve warm or cool.

Plum Pudding

A storybook fantasy come true! It's truly worth the time.

PREPARATION TIME:	25 minutes
COOKING TIME:	4–5 hours
COOLING TIME:	30 minutes
YIELD:	6–8 servings (Recipe can be doubled or cut in half.)

2 cups raisins (packed), finely chopped or ground
½ cup nuts, ground
¼ teaspoon nutmeg
½ teaspoon cinnamon
⅔ cup honey
½ cup (1 stick) butter or soy margarine, melted
½ teaspoon vanilla
4 large eggs, beaten with a fork
2 cups soft whole-wheat bread crumbs (packed)

<u>*Topping (optional)*</u>
1 cup heavy cream whipped to a hard, firm state (Hard Sauce)
or
½ recipe of Maple Cream Frosting (non-dairy), see page 136

1. Blend raisins, nuts, and spices in a large bowl.

2. Add honey, butter, vanilla, and eggs. Mix well.

3. Add bread crumbs and mix until ingredients are evenly blended.

4. Place mixture into well buttered or oiled container. (A coffee can or $1\frac{1}{2}$-pint ceramic or glass bowl will do.) Fill to no more than $1\frac{1}{2}$ inches from the top of the container.

5. Cover the top of the container with an oiled cloth held in place with a string, or with a tight covering of aluminum foil.

6. Set the container on a rack or inverted steamer in a large kettle with water reaching half-way up the sides of the container. (A crock pot with a coffee can inside also works to steam pudding.)

7. Cover the kettle and simmer for 4–5 hours. Add boiling water as needed.

8. When pudding is done (it will be firm to the touch), remove container from pan and cool for 30 minutes.

9. Loosen the pudding with a knife or spatula around edges. Invert onto a serving plate and remove can.

10. Decorate pudding with a sprig of holly for a festive touch and garnish with Hard Sauce or Maple Cream Frosting if desired.

11. Pudding may be refrigerated in the mold for several weeks. Resteam for 1 hour before unmolding and serving.

Candies,
Frostings, Glazes

Watch eyes light up when you present
these fabulous classic sweets.
A platter of old-fashioned fudge
or the sight of swirled frosting
brings out the "kid" in all of us.

Hints

🍃 Avoid making candy on wet or humid days. Humidity affects the final outcome of all candy, especially divinity.

🍃 When boiling pure maple syrup, use a very deep pot because the boiling syrup will rise up quite high as the temperature increases.

🍃 Using a candy thermometer is the easiest way to make sure that candies will turn out right. However, the old method of dropping a few drops of hot syrup in a cup of cold water until the syrup is hot enough to form a soft ball-shape works just as well. It just takes a little practice.

🍃 The candies in this book will stay fresh for several weeks if completely cooled and kept tightly covered in a cool, dry area. Divinity stores better in airtight containers lined with wax paper.

🍃 Additional sauces can be prepared by following the cream pudding recipes on pages 107–113. Add additional milk or soy milk to the mixture and cook until it is desired consistency.

🍃 Candy recipes can sometimes be modified to create frostings. Directions for these variations are included with the candy recipes.

Carob Fudge

*When my son was asked to name his own reward
for an honor roll report card,
this is what he chose.*

PREPARATION TIME: 20 minutes
YIELD: 25 pieces, 1-inch square

1 cup pure maple syrup
1 tablespoon carob powder, sifted
⅛ teaspoon sea salt
⅔ cup cream, milk, or soy milk
½ teaspoon vanilla
1 tablespoon butter or soy margarine
½ cup nuts, chopped (optional)

1. In a deep pan, combine syrup, carob powder, salt, and cream. Stir until ingredients are blended.

2. Cook on medium-high heat until soft ball-stage. (At 230°F, tiny drops of the mixture will form tadpole shapes when dropped in cold water.)

3. Remove pan from heat. Add vanilla and butter and stir until mixture is smooth and still warm.

4. Add nuts and turn mixture out onto a well-buttered plate.

5. Cut into small squares before candy completely hardens.

Variation

Carob Fudge Frosting

Follow the directions for Carob Fudge. While still warm and soft, mixture should be spread between layers and on top of a two-layer cake. Allow to run over the edges as a glaze.

Glazed Nuts

---

*These glazed nuts are a wonderfully quick holiday snack
that also makes a welcomed gift.*

PREPARATION TIME:	15 minutes
COOLING TIME:	10 minutes
YIELD:	2 cups

½ cup pure maple syrup
2 cups pecan or walnut halves

1. Oil a sheet of wax paper or a cookie sheet.

2. Cook maple syrup on medium heat in a large pan until soft ball-stage. (At 230°F, a tadpole shape will form when a small amount of syrup is dropped in cold water.)

3. Remove pan from heat. Add nuts and stir until they are coated and separate from each other.

4. Turn nuts out on an oiled surface to cool and harden.

Maple Fudge

*Here's a recipe that took a prize at our county fair.
It stood up well in competition with candies made with processed sugar.*

PREPARATION TIME: 20 minutes
YIELD: 25 pieces, 1-inch square

1 cup pure maple syrup
⅔ cup cream, milk, or soy milk
⅛ teaspoon sea salt
¼ teaspoon vanilla
1 tablespoon butter or soy margarine
½ cup nuts, chopped (optional)

1. In a deep pan, combine syrup, cream, and salt. Stir until blended.

2. Cook on medium-high heat until soft ball-stage. (At 230°F, tiny drops of the mixture will form tadpole shapes when dropped in cold water.)

3. Remove pan from heat. Add vanilla and butter, and stir until mixture is smooth and still warm.

4. Add nuts and turn mixture out onto a well-buttered plate.

5. Cut into small squares before candy completely hardens.

Variation

Maple Fudge Frosting

Follow the directions for Maple Fudge. While mixture is still warm and soft, spread it between layers and on top of a two-layer cake. Allow fudge to run over edges as a glaze.

Peanut Butter Fudge

Popular with "kids" of all ages.

PREPARATION TIME: 20 minutes
YIELD: 25 pieces, 1-inch square

⅔ cup pure maple syrup
1 teaspoon molasses
½ cup cream, milk, or soy milk
¼ teaspoon sea salt
½ teaspoon vanilla
1 tablespoon natural smooth peanut butter, unsalted*
½ cup nuts, chopped (optional)

1. In a deep pan, combine syrup, molasses, cream, and salt. Stir until blended.

2. Cook on medium-high heat until soft ball-stage. (At 230°F, tiny drops of the mixture will form tadpole shapes when dropped in cold water.)

3. Remove pan from heat. Add vanilla and peanut butter and stir until mixture is smooth and still warm.

4. Add nuts and turn mixture out onto a well-buttered plate.

5. Cut into small squares before candy completely hardens.

Variation

Peanut Butter Fudge Frosting

Follow the directions for Peanut Butter Fudge. While mixture is still warm and soft, spread it between layers and on top of a two-layer cake. Allow to run over the edges as a glaze.

---

*Chunky peanut butter may be used and optional nuts eliminated.

Divinity Candy

A truly divine confection!
This recipe won a ribbon at the county fair.

PREPARATION TIME: 20 minutes
YIELD: 2 dozen 1-inch pieces

1 cup pure maple syrup
1 large egg white, room temperature

1. In a deep pot, cook maple syrup to the firm ball-stage. (At 250–260°F, tiny drops of the syrup will form firm tadpole shapes and threads when dropped in cold water.)

2. While the syrup is cooking to this stage, prepare the egg white. Beat it in a small bowl until soft peaks form. Pack beaten white into a $\frac{1}{2}$-cup measure. (Whether making Divinity Candy or frosting, you must measure accurately to ensure success. Use only the measured amount of egg whites. Discard any extra whites.) Transfer the $\frac{1}{2}$ cup of white to a medium-sized bowl.

3. When syrup has reached the firm ball-stage, gradually add it to the egg white while continuing to beat.

4. Beat on high speed until the mixture forms a mass around the beaters.

5. Put the mixer on slowest speed and lift to release candy from beaters.

6. Beat by hand until mixture loses its gloss and holds its shape.

7. Work quickly at this point to spoon mixture by teaspoons onto a slightly oiled cookie sheet or waxed paper.

8. Top with pecan or walnut halves, gently pressing nuts into place.

Variation

Divinity Frosting

Follow the directions for Divinity Candy. Use 2 egg whites to make 1 cup of packed, beaten whites. Stop the electric mixer at the point when the mixture forms a mass around the beaters. Use the mixture to frost a two-layer cake.

Cream Cheese Frosting

A flavorful complement for carrot, banana, date, and spice cakes.

PREPARATION TIME: 10 minutes
YIELD: 1½ cups (enough to frost 1 two-layer cake, 2 loaves, or 32 cupcakes. Recipe may be halved.)

2 tablespoons butter, room temperature
¼ cup honey
8 ounces cream cheese, room temperature
½ teaspoon vanilla
¼ cup finely chopped nuts for topping (optional)

1. Cream together butter, honey, and cream cheese.

2. Add vanilla and mix to blend.

3. Spread on a cooled cake. Top with nuts if desired.

Pralines

Easy, never-fail technique for turning out a scrumptious Southern favorite.

PREPARATION TIME: 20 minutes
YIELD: 25 patties, 2 inches in diameter

½ cup pure maple syrup
2 cups pecans, whole or chopped

1. Cook maple syrup in a deep pot on medium-high heat until soft ball-stage. (At 230°F, a tadpole shape will form when a small amount of syrup is dropped in cold water.)

2. Remove pot from heat. Add pecans and stir until nuts are coated. When mixture is cool enough to touch, form small patties. (If the candy hardens too quickly, dampen hands with water and continue.)

3. Place patties on lightly oiled cookie sheet or oiled wax paper to completely cool.

Variation

New Orleans Pralines

Follow the directions for making Pralines except decrease the ½ cup maple syrup to 3 tablespoons and add 1 tablespoon molasses and ¼ cup heavy cream before cooking the mixture.

Maple Sugar

*A sprinkle of this unique homemade "sugar" is all that's needed
on cookies, custards and fruits.
(Keeps almost indefinitely in an air-tight container.)*

PREPARATION TIME: 10 minutes
YIELD: ¼ cup (enough to sprinkle on 2 dozen 2-inch
cookies or 8–10 half-cup servings of fruit.
Recipe may be doubled.)

¼ cup pure maple syrup

1. Cook maple syrup in a small pan to soft ball-stage. (At 230°F, a tadpole shape will form when a small amount of syrup is dropped in cold water.)

2. Remove pan from heat.

3. Place the bottom of the pan in cold water.

4. Stir until syrup turns soft and smooth.

5. Continue stirring until mixture has the consistency of sugar.

6. Use sparingly to sprinkle over cookies, custard, or fruits.

Variation

Maple Brown Sugar

Follow the directions for Maple Sugar. When the mixture begins to crystallize, add 1 teaspoon molasses. Continue stirring until mixture becomes dry and powdery.

Marshmallows

Watch the amazing transformation of maple syrup to a white, fluffy candy. (Marshmallows can also be made with honey, but maple is the way to go.)

PREPARATION: 25 minutes
YIELD: 2 dozen

1 tablespoon (1 envelope) unflavored gelatin
1/4 cup water
1/4 teaspoon vanilla
pinch of sea salt
1/2 cup pure maple syrup
1 cup shredded unsweetened coconut or finely ground nuts

1. Combine gelatin, water, vanilla, and salt in a small cup. Stir and set aside.

2. Cook syrup in a medium-sized pan on medium heat until soft ball-stage. (At 230°F, tiny drops of the mixture will form tadpole shapes when dropped in cold water.)

3. Remove pan from heat, add gelatin mixture, and stir to dissolve.

4. Transfer mixture to a medium-sized bowl. Beat at high speed for 5–8 minutes or until mixture turns white, forms peaks, and clings in a mass to the beaters.

5. Put the mixer on slowest speed and lift to release candy from beaters.

6. Drop mixture by teaspoons on wax paper sprinkled with coconut or ground nuts.

7. Sprinkle tops with coconut or ground nuts, and allow Marshmallows to set.

8. May be eaten immediately or stored in the refrigerator or at room temperature in an airtight container for up to three weeks.

Variation

Pecan Log

Follow the directions for Marshmallows. Drop entire mixture on wax paper sprinkled with ground pecans. Shape into a log. Sprinkle evenly with remaining nuts. Allow log to set before slicing.

Butter Cream Frosting

This rich, smooth mixture is our answer to powdered sugar frostings. Flour is the "secret" ingredient that makes it work.

PREPARATION TIME: 5 minutes
YIELD: 3½ cups (enough to frost 1 two-layer cake or 48 cupcakes. Recipe may be halved.)

½ cup (1 stick) butter or soy margarine, room temperature
1 cup honey
1 teaspoon vanilla
1½ cups unbleached flour, unsifted

1. Cream butter, honey, and vanilla.

2. Beat until smooth.

3. Gradually add flour, continuing to beat until mixture is well-blended and smooth.

4. This frosting (and its variations) may be refrigerated up to 1 week. Bring to room temperature before using.

Variations

Lemon Cream Frosting

Follow the recipe for Butter Cream Frosting except eliminate vanilla and replace with lemon extract. Add ½ teaspoon grated lemon rind.

Maple Cream Frosting

Follow the recipe for Butter Cream Frosting except substitute pure maple syrup for honey and eliminate vanilla.

Orange Cream Frosting

Follow the recipe for Butter Cream Frosting except eliminate vanilla and replace with orange extract. Add ½ teasoon grated orange rind.

Non-Dairy Whipped Topping

A quick yet delicate alternative to whipped cream.
Try it on custard pies, puddings, shortcakes, and fruit.

PREPARATION TIME: 5 minutes
YIELD: 1½ cups, 6 servings (2 tablespoons each)

2 large egg whites, cold
½ teaspoon vanilla
1 tablespoon honey

1. In a medium-sized bowl, beat egg whites until soft peaks form.

2. Add vanilla and honey. Beat mixture until it is well blended.

3. Just before serving, beat topping vigorously by hand until peaks form.

4. Best when served immediately. May also be refrigerated for up to 1 hour. Remove from refrigerator and beat vigorously by hand until peaks reform.

Whipped Cream Frosting

A fantastic, firm frosting that maintains its shape for several hours.

PREPARATION TIME:	10 minutes
CHILLING TIME:	30–60 minutes
YIELD:	$1\frac{1}{2}$ cups (enough to frost a 9-inch one-layer cake or 18 cupcakes. Recipe may be doubled.)

½ teaspoon unflavored gelatin
1 tablespoon water
1 cup (½-pint carton) heavy cream
1 tablespoon honey or pure maple syrup
½ teaspoon vanilla (omit if maple syrup is used)

1. Mix gelatin and water in a cup.

2. Place cup in bowl of hot water until gelatin is dissolved and mixture is clear. Set aside.

3. Whip cream until it is firm.

4. Add honey or maple syrup, gelatin, and vanilla if honey is the sweetener. Beat until well blended.

5. Refrigerate 30 minutes to 1 hour before using.

Carob Cream Frosting

A candy-like frosting that transforms a simple cake into a luscious dessert.

PREPARATION TIME: 5 minutes
YIELD: 3½ cups (enough to frost 1 two-layer cake or 48 cupcakes. Recipe may be halved.)

½ *cup (1 stick) butter or soy margarine, room temperature*
1 cup honey
1 teaspoon vanilla
¼ *cup carob powder, sifted*
1¼ *cups unbleached flour, unsifted*

1. Cream butter, honey, and vanilla.

2. Beat until smooth.

3. Gradually add carob and flour, continuing to beat until the mixture is well-blended and smooth.

4. Frosting may be refrigerated for up to 1 week. Bring to room temperature before spreading.

Variation

Carob Mint Frosting

Follow the recipe for regular Carob Cream Frosting except eliminate vanilla and replace with ½ teaspoon peppermint extract.

Pecan Frosting

The richest of the frostings; a must for German Carob Cake (see page 11).

PREPARATION TIME:	25 minutes
COOLING TIME:	40 minutes
YIELD:	3½ cups (enough to frost 1 two-layer cake or 48 cupcakes. Recipe may be halved.)

½ cup (1 stick) butter or soy margarine
1 cup honey
1 cup (½-pint carton) heavy cream or soy milk
4 large egg yolks
1 teaspoon vanilla
1 cup pecans, finely chopped

1. In a medium-sized saucepan, combine butter, honey, and cream.

2. Cook on medium-high heat until mixture is hot and steamy.

3. Gradually stir several tablespoons of hot mixture into yolks.

4. Return all to pan.

5. Continue cooking and stirring constantly about 10–12 minutes until mixture is thick and bubbly.

6. Add vanilla and pecans. Stir to mix.

7. Remove pan from the stove and cool thoroughly before frosting cake.

Fruit
Cream Cheese Frosting

Brings a touch of color to Angel Food Cake (see page 22),
Cool-Center Crêpes (see page 167), or Basic Yellow Cake (see page 8).

PREPARATION TIME: 20 minutes
CHILLING TIME: 15 minutes
YIELD: 3½ cups (enough to frost 1 two-layer cake or
48 cupcakes. Recipe may be halved.)

1 teaspoon unflavored gelatin
2 tablespoons water
1 cup (½-pint carton) heavy cream
8 ounces cream cheese, room temperature
½ cup honey
2 cups fresh fruit or a 16-ounce can of fruit,
finely chopped and well-drained

1. Mix gelatin and water in a cup.

2. Place the cup in a bowl of hot water until gelatin is dissolved and mixture is clear. Set aside.

3. Whip cream in a medium-sized bowl until it is firm.

4. Add gelatin and beat mixture for 30 seconds until blended.

5. Refrigerate for 15 minutes.

6. In another bowl, combine cream cheese, honey, and fruit. Whip until mixture is smooth.

7. Add whipped cream to cream cheese mixture and blend.

Fruit Glaze

*A simple way to add color and fruity flavor
to shortcakes, cheesecakes, and waffles.*

PREPARATION TIME: 15 minutes
COOLING TIME: 20 minutes
YIELD: 3 cups

$2\frac{1}{2}$ tablespoons arrowroot or cornstarch
$\frac{1}{2}$ cup fruit juice or water
$\frac{2}{3}$ cup honey
$\frac{1}{8}$ teaspoon sea salt
$\frac{1}{4}$ teaspoon lemon juice
$1\frac{1}{2}$ cups fresh fruit or a 16-ounce can of fruit, drained

1. Combine arrowroot and juice in a cup. Mix thoroughly and set aside.

2. In a medium-sized pan, add honey, salt, lemon juice, and arrowroot mixture.

3. Cook mixture over medium heat for about 5 minutes, stirring constantly until mixture is thick.

4. Remove pan from heat and cool mixture completely.

5. Add fruit and mix well.

6. Spread on shortcakes, cheesecakes, or waffles.

Lemon Sauce

The traditional gingerbread topping.
Its tangy flavor serves many other purposes.

PREPARATION TIME: 15 minutes
COOLING TIME: 15 minutes
YIELD: 1 cup

$1\frac{1}{2}$ tablespoons arrowroot or cornstarch
$\frac{1}{2}$ cup water
$\frac{1}{2}$ cup honey
1 tablespoon lemon juice
$\frac{1}{8}$ teaspoon sea salt
2 tablespoons butter or soy margarine
1 teaspoon grated lemon rind (optional)

1. Combine arrowroot and water in a cup. Mix thoroughly and set aside.

2. In a medium-sized pan, combine honey, lemon juice, and salt. Cook over medium heat until mixture is hot.

3. Add arrowroot mixture. Cook for about 5 minutes, stirring constantly until mixture is thick.

4. Remove mixture from heat, add butter, and then cool completely.

5. Serve as a topping over Gingerbread (see page 16), Angel Food Cake (see page 22), fruit salad, rice or bread pudding.

Variations

Orange Sauce

Follow directions for Lemon Sauce. Replace water with orange juice and reduce lemon juice to ½ teaspoon.

Pineapple Sauce

Follow directions for Lemon Sauce. Replace water with pineapple juice and reduce lemon juice to ½ teaspoon.

Carob Syrup

A rich, dark topping for that final touch.

PREPARATION TIME: 15 minutes
YIELD: 1 pint or 2 cups

½ cup carob powder
1 tablespoon unbleached flour, unsifted
⅛ teaspoon sea salt
1 cup honey
1 cup water
1 teaspoon vanilla

1. Sift carob powder, flour, and salt into a small pan. Add honey and stir until a thick, smooth paste forms.

2. Gradually add water, stirring after each addition.

3. Cook on medium heat, stirring constantly for 10–15 minutes until mixture is desired thickness.

4. Remove from heat. Add vanilla, stir, and cool.

5. Pour into pint jar and store in the refrigerator for up to 3 weeks.

6. Stir before serving over ice cream, Angel Food Cake (see page 22), Cream Puffs (see page 73), or fruits.

Cooling Desserts

A parade of light, refreshing desserts
to spotlight any occasion:
fancy gelatin molds
frosty treats on a stick
finale of luscious fruit salad

Hints

❧   When beating egg whites, be sure the bowl and beaters are completely free of oil or specks of egg yolk or the whites cannot be beaten stiff.

❧   Fold ingredients into beaten egg whites with a rubber spatula by cutting down through the center of the egg whites, across the bottom of the bowl and up the side. Turn the bowl about a quarter turn. Repeat the action until the mixture is evenly blended.

❧   Old-fashioned wooden popsicle sticks can be purchased at craft and hobby stores. They can be washed and reused.

❧   Small plastic drinking cups make good reusable molds for frozen pops.

❧   Frozen banana pops are easy to make: make a horizontal cut through the middle of a ripe banana; insert wooden stick into flat, cut end; place banana on foil and freeze for several hours.

❧   Since mousse contains gelatin, it makes elegant frozen desserts. Follow the directions for frozen pops or freeze the mousse in its container.

❧   When making fruit salad, combine fruits that are similar and then add one fruit for contrast. For example—orange, kiwi, grapefruit, and banana; watermelon, cantaloupe, honeydew, and blueberries or strawberries. To citrus or banana and apple salad, add chopped dates and sprinkle with walnut pieces or coconut. Toss with a cup of yogurt or, better yet, Honey Lime Dressing (see page 152). Chill and serve.

Gelatin Dessert

Its versatility complements any meal.

PREPARATION TIME: 5 minutes
CHILLING TIME: 3–5 hours
YIELD: 4 servings

2 cups fruit juice*
1 tablespoon (1 envelope) unflavored gelatin**

1. Measure fruit juice into a medium-sized pan.

2. Add gelatin and mix until it is dissolved.

3. Cook mixture over medium heat, stirring constantly. *Do not boil.*

4. Pour mixture into a bowl or mold and chill for several hours before serving.*

5. Top with fruit or whipped cream

---

*For gelatin that compares to the sweetness of the commercial product, decrease juice to $1\frac{3}{4}$ cups and add $\frac{1}{4}$ cup of honey.

**For a firmer, more solid mold, add an additional $\frac{1}{2}$ tablespoon of gelatin. Brush the molds lightly with oil before pouring in gelatin mixture. Chopped fruit or nuts may be added when gelatin mixture is partially set.

Date Whip

An almost instant, non-dairy dream for quick entertaining.

PREPARATION TIME: 10 minutes
YIELD: 4–6 servings

1 cup pitted dates
2 large egg whites, cold
⅛ teaspoon sea salt
¼ teaspoon vanilla
½ teaspoon lemon juice
3 tablespoons honey, room temperature
2 tablespoons ground walnuts or pecans

1. Chop dates and set aside.

2. In a medium-sized bowl, beat cold egg whites until stiff peaks form.

3. Add sea salt, vanilla, and lemon juice one at a time, beating slightly after each addition.

4. Add honey and beat only until soft peaks form.

5. Add dates and beat slightly just until blended. Do not overbeat.

6. Spoon dessert into serving dishes and top with ground nuts.

7. Serve immediately or chill not more than 30 minutes.

Variations

Prune Whip

Follow directions for Date Whip except substitute 1 cup of chopped, pitted prunes for dates.

Fresh Fruit Whip

Follow the directions for Date Whip except substitute 1 cup fresh, chopped peaches or strawberries, drained, for dates. Nut topping is optional.

Carob Whip

*An excellent way to introduce your family and friends
to the fine taste of carob.*

PREPARATION TIME: 10 minutes
YIELD: 4–6 servings

3 tablespoons honey, room temperature
¼ teaspoon vanilla
2 teaspoons carob powder
2 large egg whites, cold
⅛ teaspoon sea salt
2 tablespoons ground walnuts or pecans

1. Combine honey, vanilla, and carob powder in a small bowl. Mix until a thick paste is formed. Set aside.

2. In a medium-sized bowl, beat egg whites with salt until stiff peaks form.

3. Add carob mixture to egg whites and beat only until blended. Do not overbeat.

4. Spoon dessert into serving dishes and top with ground nuts.

5. Serve immediately or chill for no longer than 30 minutes.

Coffee Whip

Just a hint of coffee creates this subtle, smooth treat.

PREPARATION TIME: 10 minutes
YIELD: 4–6 servings

½ teaspoon instant grain coffee
⅛ teaspoon cinnamon
½ teaspoon cold water
2 large egg whites, cold
⅛ teaspoon sea salt
3 tablespoons honey, room temperature
2 tablespoons ground walnuts or pecans

1. In a small bowl or cup, combine coffee, cinnamon, and cold water. Stir until coffee is dissolved. Set aside.

2. In a medium-sized bowl, beat egg whites with salt until stiff peaks form.

3. Add coffee mixture and beat only until blended, about 10 seconds.

4. Add the honey and beat only until blended, about 10 seconds.

5. Spoon dessert into serving dishes and top with ground nuts.

6. Serve immediately or chill for no longer than 30 minutes.

Fruit Salad With Honey Lime Dressing

Fresh fruit in season makes a satisfying, quick salad-dessert.

PREPARATION TIME:	30 minutes
CHILLING TIME:	30 minutes
YIELD:	6–8 servings of fruit salad; $\frac{3}{4}$ cup dressing

Fruit Salad
*2 quarts peeled, cored, and diced fresh fruit
(add banana just before serving)*

Dressing
2 tablespoons lime juice
2 tablespoons honey
$\frac{1}{4}$ cup oil
$\frac{1}{4}$ teaspoon prepared mustard
$\frac{1}{8}$ teaspoon sea salt
$\frac{1}{4}$ teaspoon paprika (optional)
1 teaspoon poppy seeds (optional)

1. Blend all dressing ingredients in a mixer or blender on high speed.

2. Pour immediately over fruit or refrigerate to thicken.

Vanilla Ice Cream

*Homemade ice cream has always been a highlight
at social and family gatherings.*

PREPARATION TIME: 25 minutes
FREEZING TIME: 30 minutes (approximate)
YIELD: 1 gallon

*6 large eggs
1 cup honey
2 cups (two ½-pint cartons) heavy cream
¼ teaspoon sea salt
2 tablespoons vanilla
milk*

1. Separate eggs, placing whites in a medium-sized bowl and yolks in a small container.

2. Beat egg whites until soft peaks form. Set aside.

3. Combine honey, cream, and salt in a medium-sized pan. Cook on medium heat until mixture begins to steam. *Do not boil.*

4. Add several tablespoons of the hot mixture to egg yolks.

5. Add egg yolk mixture to the remaining mixture in the pan.

6. Continue heating and stirring until mixture thickens only enough to coat a wooden spoon. (Remove any cooked egg particles.)

7. Remove mixture from heat and add vanilla.

8. Strain and pour into a large bowl.

9. Add egg whites and beat until mixture is foamy.

10. Pour mixture into gallon container of an ice cream freezer.

11. Fill the rest of the container with milk until $\frac{3}{4}$ full.

12. Freeze according to manufacturer's instructions.

Variations

Fruit Ice Cream

Follow the directions for Vanilla Ice Cream. Add 2 cups crushed fruit such as banana or strawberry and increase honey by $\frac{1}{4}$ cup.

Carob Ice Cream

Follow the directions for Vanilla Ice Cream. Sift $\frac{1}{4}$ cup carob powder into honey mixture in saucepan before heating. Increase honey by $\frac{1}{3}$ cup and decrease vanilla by 1 tablespoon.

Vanilla Soy-Milk Ice Cream

A custard-like, non-dairy version of America's favorite dessert.

PREPARATION TIME: 25 minutes
FREEZING TIME: 40 minutes
YIELD: 1½ quarts

3 large eggs
½ cup honey
⅛ teaspoon sea salt
1 quart soy milk (non-flavored variety)
1 tablespoon vanilla

1. Separate eggs, placing whites in a medium-sized bowl and yolks in a small container or cup.

2. Beat egg whites until soft peaks form. Set aside.

3. Combine honey, salt, and 1 cup of soy milk in a medium-sized pan.

4. Cook on medium heat until mixture begins to steam. *Do not boil.*

5. Add several tablespoons of the hot mixture to egg yolks. Stir and return all to pan.

6. Continue heating and stirring until mixture thickens only enough to coat a wooden spoon. (Remove any cooked egg particles.)

7. Remove from heat and add vanilla and remainder of soy milk.

8. Strain and pour into a large bowl.

9. Add egg whites and beat until mixture is foamy.

10. Pour mixture into ice cream freezer container, and freeze according to manufacturer's instructions.

Variations

Carob Soy-Milk Ice Cream

Follow directions for Vanilla Soy-Milk Ice Cream. In addition, increase honey by 1 tablespoon and sift 2 tablespoons carob powder into honey mixture before heating. Decrease vanilla to $\frac{1}{2}$ tablespoon.

Fruit Soy-Milk Ice Cream

Follow directions for Vanilla Soy-Milk Ice Cream. Before freezing, add 1 cup crushed fruit such as banana or strawberry. Increase honey by 1 tablespoon.

Frozen Pops

These pops have the same smooth consistency as the commercial variety.

PREPARATION TIME:	15 minutes
FREEZING TIME:	24 hours
YIELD:	12–15 cubes, 6 molds (Recipe may be doubled.)

¼ cup honey
½ tablespoon (½ envelope) unflavored gelatin
1¾ cups fruit juice

1. In a medium-sized saucepan, combine honey, gelatin, and juice. Stir to mix and dissolve ingredients.

2. Cook until mixture steams. *Do not boil.*

3. Pour mixture into a small pitcher for ease of transfer into special molds or ice trays.

4. When mixture is partially frozen, insert toothpicks in the centers for handles.

5. Freeze 24 hours for best results.

6. Remove pops by partially submerging the trays or molds in hot water for a few seconds. A sharp knife is helpful in loosening the edges.

Variations

Cream Pops

Follow directions for Frozen Pops except substitute ¾ cup milk, soy milk, or cream for juice.

Fudge Pops

Follow directions for Frozen Pops except add $\frac{1}{4}$ teaspoon vanilla and 2 tablespoons carob powder. Use milk or soy milk instead of juice. Strain mixture into a small pitcher before filling molds or ice trays.

Pudding Pops

Follow directions for Frozen Pops except add $\frac{1}{2}$ teaspoon vanilla, use milk instead of juice, and add 2 large beaten egg yolks. *Do not boil.* Strain mixture into a small pitcher before filling molds or ice trays.

Fruit Mousse

My Lady's favorite—light and fruity.

PREPARATION TIME:	30 minutes
CHILLING TIME:	2 hours
YIELD:	10 half-cup servings

1 tablespoon (1 envelope) unflavored gelatin
$\frac{1}{4}$ cup water
$\frac{1}{2}$ cup honey
$1\frac{1}{4}$ cups unsweetened fruit juice (orange, pineapple, grape, etc.)
1 teaspoon lemon juice
$\frac{1}{8}$ teaspoon sea salt
3 egg yolks, slightly beaten
3 egg whites, chilled
1 cup heavy cream, whipped
1 teaspoon grated orange or lemon rind (optional)

1. Mix gelatin and water in a small bowl.

2. Place the small bowl in a large bowl of hot water until gelatin is dissolved and mixture is clear. Set aside.

3. Combine honey, fruit juice, lemon juice, and salt in a small pan.

4. Cook over medium heat until mixture is hot.

5. Gradually stir several teaspoons of hot mixture into slightly beaten egg yolks.

6. Add egg yolk mixture to remaining mixture in pan.

7. Continue to cook mixture over medium heat, stirring constantly until mixture is smooth and slightly thick.

8. Remove pan from heat. Remove any cooked egg particles.

9. Add gelatin, stirring until evenly mixed.

10. Transfer mixture to a large bowl and chill it for 1 hour or until it is partially set.

11. Beat egg whites until they are stiff.

12. Fold beaten egg whites, grated rind, and then whipped cream into chilled mixture until it is smooth and well mixed.

13. Turn mixture into pudding glasses and refrigerate 1 hour or until firm.

Maple Mousse

Perfect for a special occasion.

PREPARATION TIME: 30 minutes
CHILLING TIME: 2 hours
YIELD: 10 half-cup servings

1 tablespoon (1 envelope) unflavored gelatin
¼ cup water
¾ cup pure maple syrup
¾ cup milk
¼ teaspoon sea salt
3 egg yolks, slightly beaten
3 egg whites, chilled
1 cup (½-pint carton) heavy cream, whipped

1. Mix gelatin and water in a small bowl.

2. Place the small bowl in a large bowl of hot water until gelatin is dissolved and mixture is clear. Set aside.

3. Combine syrup, milk, and salt in a small pan. Cook over medium heat until mixture is hot.

4. Gradually stir several tablespoons of hot mixture into beaten egg yolks.

5. Add egg yolk mixture to the remaining mixture in the pan.

6. Continue to cook over medium heat, stirring constantly until mixture is smooth and slightly thick.

7. Remove pan from heat, remove any cooked egg particles, and add dissolved gelatin, stirring until evenly mixed.

8. Transfer mixture to a large bowl and chill for 1 hour or until it is partially set.

9. Beat egg whites until they are stiff.

10. Fold in stiffly-beaten egg whites then whipped cream until mixture is smooth and well-mixed.

11. Turn mousse into pudding glasses and refrigerate 1 hour or until it is firm.

Maple Nut Whip

Simple ingredients produce amazing results.

PREPARATION TIME: 5 minutes
YIELD: 4–6 servings

2 large egg whites, chilled
$\frac{1}{8}$ teaspoon sea salt
3 tablespoons pure maple syrup, cold
2 tablespoons ground walnuts or pecans

1. In a medium-sized bowl, beat the cold egg whites until stiff peaks form.

2. Add sea salt and gradually add maple syrup while beating. Beat only until soft peaks form (about 15 seconds).

3. Spoon into serving dishes and top with ground nuts.

4. Serve immediately or chill not more than 30 minutes.

Carob Mousse

A rich and luscious finale.

PREPARATION TIME:	30 minutes
CHILLING TIME:	2 hours
YIELD:	10 half-cup servings

1 tablespoon (1 envelope) unflavored gelatin
¼ cup water
¾ cup honey
¼ cup carob powder, sifted
¼ teaspoon sea salt
¾ cup milk
3 egg yolks, slightly beaten
3 egg whites, chilled
1 cup (½-pint carton) heavy cream, whipped

1. Mix gelatin and water in a small bowl.

2. Place small bowl in a large bowl of hot water until gelatin is dissolved and mixture is clear. Set aside.

3. Combine honey, carob powder, and salt in a small pan and mix until a thick paste forms.

4. Stir in milk and cook mixture over medium heat until it is hot.

5. Gradually stir several tablespoons of hot mixture into the beaten egg yolks.

6. Add egg yolk mixture to the remaining mixture in the pan.

7. Continue to cook mixture over medium heat, stirring constantly until mixture is smooth and slightly thick.

8. Remove pan from heat. (Remove any cooked egg particles.)

9. Add gelatin, stirring until ingredients are evenly mixed.

10. Transfer mixture to a large bowl and chill for 1 hour or until it is partially set.

11. Beat egg whites until they are stiff.

12. Fold beaten egg whites then whipped cream into chilled mixture until it is smooth and well-mixed.

13. Turn into pudding glasses and refrigerate 1 hour or until firm.

Peanut Butter Mousse

An old stand-by in an elegant setting.

PREPARATION TIME: 30 minutes
CHILLING TIME: 2 hours
YIELD: 10 half-cup servings

1 tablespoon (1 envelope) unflavored gelatin
¼ cup water
¾ cup honey
⅓ cup unsalted natural peanut butter, smooth
¼ teaspoon sea salt
¾ cup milk
3 egg yolks, slightly beaten
3 egg whites, chilled
1 teaspoon vanilla
1 cup (½-pint carton) heavy cream, whipped

1. Mix gelatin and water in a small bowl.

2. Place small bowl in a large bowl of hot water until gelatin is dissolved and mixture is clear. Set aside.

3. Combine honey, peanut butter, salt, and milk in a small pan.

4. Cook over medium heat until mixture is hot.

5. Gradually stir several tablespoons of hot mixture into beaten egg yolks.

6. Add the egg yolk mixture to the remaining mixture in the pan.

7. Continue to cook over medium heat, stirring constantly until mixture is smooth and slightly thick.

8. Remove from heat. (Remove any cooked egg particles.)

9. Add gelatin and vanilla, stirring until ingredients are evenly mixed.

10. Transfer mixture to a large bowl and chill for 1 hour or until it is partially set.

11. Beat egg whites until they are stiff.

12. Fold beaten egg whites then whipped cream into chilled mixture until it is smooth and well-mixed.

13. Turn mousse into pudding glasses and refrigerate 1 hour or until firm.

Cool-Center Crêpes

Ordinary ingredients produce this impressive delicacy.
Keep some on hand in the freezer for unexpected guests.

PREPARATION TIME:	10 minutes
COOKING TIME:	20 minutes
CHILLING TIME:	2 hours
YIELD:	10–12 servings

1 cup unbleached flour, unsifted
½ cup whole-wheat pastry flour, unsifted
¾ cup milk or soy milk
¾ cup cold water
3 large egg yolks
½ tablespoon honey*
4 tablespoons butter or soy margarine, melted

1. Sift the dry ingredients together twice. Set aside.

2. Place liquid ingredients except for melted butter or soy margarine in a blender jar in the order listed above.

3. Add sifted flour and then melted butter or soy margarine.

4. Cover jar and blend at highest speed for 1 minute.

5. Remove cover and run a spatula around sides of jar to loosen flour. Blend a few seconds more.

6. Cover and refrigerate at least 2 hours. (Batter may be made the day before and refrigerated overnight.)

7. Drop batter by $\frac{1}{4}$ cups onto a hot, oiled crêpe pan or a skillet with slanted sides. Turn pan so as to evenly coat the bottom.

8. Check for doneness by lifting an edge of the crêpe with a spatula. When crêpe is lightly golden, turn it using fingers and spatula.

9. Remove crêpes to a serving plate, refrigerate or freeze, separating crêpes with wax paper.

10. Crêpes may be stuffed with ricotta cheese or a cool confection such as ice cream and topped with fruit, nuts, or whipped cream.

---

*To make dinner crêpes, omit the honey.

Waffles and Ice Cream

Easy to make from readily-available ingredients.
Top with fruit and whipped cream and serve as an evening dessert.

PREPARATION TIME:	10 minutes
COOKING TIME:	25 minutes
YIELD:	12*

1 cup whole-wheat pastry flour, unsifted
1 cup unbleached flour, unsifted
1 teaspoon baking powder
½ teaspoon sea salt
¼ cup oil
2 tablespoons honey
1 large egg
2 cups milk or soy milk

1. In a large bowl, stir the dry ingredients until they are evenly mixed.

2. Add oil, honey, and egg and mix.

3. Add milk, 1 cup at a time.

4. Blend with an electric mixer until batter is smooth.

5. Pour onto hot, lightly oiled waffle iron following manufacturer's directions. (Pour batter onto an oiled griddle to make pancakes.)

6. Cook waffles until they are brown and firm.

7. Top with ice cream (see pages 153–156).

---

*Extra waffles for the freezer can be made by doubling the recipe. Place each waffle between layers of wax paper. Secure in a plastic bag and freeze. Individual waffles can be put in the toaster still frozen.

Beverages

Here are the perfect liquid companions
for those festive moments.
Serve in your most elegant glasses and cups
to double the enjoyment.
There is nothing so inviting as an attractive,
colorful punch bowl at a social gathering.
A mug filled with hot, steamy refreshment
on a cold winter's night
is instant bliss.

Hints

❧ An ice ring helps to cool and dress up a punch bowl. An 8-inch gelatin mold makes an attractive ring. Fill a 2- to 6-cup mold with juice and freeze for about an hour or until the juice is partially frozen. Decorate the ring by carefully pressing bits of lemon and lime rinds along with strawberries into the frozen juice. Return mold to freezer and freeze for at least 6 hours. Run warm water over the mold to release the ring. As the ice ring melts, the fruit bits add to the flavor of the punch.

❧ A 12-ounce can of frozen juice concentrate makes 6 cups of juice. Bottled juices work as well as frozen concentrates.

Rose Punch

A festive party-pleaser for all occasions.

PREPARATION TIME: 15 minutes
YIELD: 40 half-cup servings

1 cup hot water
4 mint tea bags
1 cup honey
4 tablespoons ($\frac{1}{4}$ cup) lemon juice
2 cups unsweetened grape juice
6 cups unsweetened orange juice
6 cups unsweetened pineapple juice
4 cups (1 quart) seltzer or sparkling spring water

1. Steep tea in hot water for 5 minutes. Set aside.

2. In a medium-sized pan, combine the honey and lemon juice. Heat and stir until mixture is thin. *Do not boil.*

3. Combine all ingredients in a punch bowl. Stir.

4. Place an ice ring (see page 172) in center of punch bowl if desired.

5. Add orange or lemon slices to punch for color.

Golden Punch

The perfect complement for cake and delicate danties.

PREPARATION TIME: 15 minutes
YIELD: 40 half-cup servings

1 cup hot water
4 mint tea bags
½ cup honey
4 tablespoons (¼ cup) lemon juice
2 cups unsweetened apple juice
6 cups unsweetened orange juice
6 cups unsweetened pineapple juice
4 cups (1 quart) seltzer or sparkling spring water

1. Steep tea in hot water for 5 minutes. Set aside.

2. In a medium-sized pan, combine honey and lemon juice. Heat and stir until the mixture is thin. Do not boil.

3. Combine all ingredients in a punch bowl. Stir.

4. Place an ice ring (see page 172) in center of punch bowl if desired.

5. Add orange or lemon slices to punch for color.

Holiday Punch (Wassail)

Deck the halls with boughs of holly
and make a batch of this traditional winter's brew.

PREPARATION TIME: 15 minutes
YIELD: 26 half-cup servings

4 tablespoons ($\frac{1}{4}$ cup) lemon juice
$\frac{1}{2}$ cup honey
6 cups unsweetened apple juice
1 cinnamon stick
6 cups unsweetened pineapple juice

1. In a large pan, combine lemon juice, honey, apple juice, and cinnamon stick.

2. Cook and stir mixture on medium heat until it begins to steam. *Do not boil.*

3. Reduce heat and cover. Simmer for 5 minutes.

4. Add pineapple juice, stir, cover, and simmer for an additional 5 minutes.

5. Remove cinnamon stick and serve punch hot.

Milk Shake I

An any time, daytime, nighttime treat.

PREPARATION: 5 minutes
YIELD: 5 half-cup servings

2 medium-sized ripe bananas, sliced
or 1 cup fresh strawberries, blackberries, or blueberries
2 tablespoons honey
½ teaspoon vanilla (optional)
1½ cups milk or soy milk*

1. Combine fruit, honey, and vanilla in a blender.

2. Blend ingredients for 5 seconds until they are puréed.

3. Add milk and blend until smooth.

---

*A cup of ice cream can be added (step 4) for a thicker, richer texture.

Milk Shake II

Look no further! You've found the thickest of the thick!

PREPARATION: 5 minutes
YIELD: 4 half-cup servings

1½ cups frozen fruit, unsweetened
(bananas, strawberries, blackberries, peaches, or blueberries)
¼ teaspoon vanilla (optional)
1 cup milk or soy milk
2 tablespoons honey

1. Combine any fruit or combination of fruits, vanilla, and milk in a blender.

2. Blend ingredients until they are puréed.

3. Add honey and blend until thick and smooth.

Smoothie

This icy cooler lives up to its name.

PREPARATION TIME: 5 minutes
YIELD: 5 half-cup servings

*1 cup fresh fruit (sliced bananas,
strawberries, peaches, blueberries, or blackberries)*
2 tablespoons honey
¼ teaspoon vanilla (optional)
½ cup juice (apple, pineapple, or orange)
2 cups crushed ice or 8–10 ice cubes

1. Combine fruit, honey, and vanilla in a blender.

2. Blend for 5 seconds until ingredients are puréed.

3. Add remaining ingredients and blend until mix is smooth and icy.

Mocha Shake

Two winning flavors, carob and coffee,
team up to produce a marvelous beverage.

PREPARATION TIME: 10 minutes
YIELD: 4 half-cup servings

1 teaspoon carob powder
2 cups milk or soy milk
2½ teaspoons instant grain coffee
3 tablespoons honey
1 teaspoon vanilla

1. In a small cup, combine carob powder and 1 tablespoon milk.

2. Stir until carob is thoroughly dissolved.

3. Pour remaining milk, carob mixture, and remaining ingredients into a blender.

4. Blend until foamy.

Variation

Iced Mocha

Follow directions for Mocha Shake, adding 6 ice cubes or a cup of crushed ice in step 3. Blend to desired consistency.

Cappuccino Shake

This is a delicious American version of an Italian classic.

PREPARATION TIME: 10 minutes
YIELD: 4 half-cup servings

2 cups milk or soy milk
2$\frac{1}{2}$ teaspoons instant grain coffee
3 tablespoons honey
1 teaspoon vanilla
$\frac{1}{4}$ teaspoon cinnamon

1. In a medium-sized saucepan, heat milk until it begins to steam. *Do not boil.*

2. Pour milk into a blender and add remaining ingredients.

3. Blend until foamy.

Variation

Iced Cappuccino

Combine ingredients for Cappuccino Shake in the blender along with 6 ice cubes or 1 cup of crushed ice. Blend to desired consistency.

Carob Drink

A healthier version of a traditional favorite.

PREPARATION TIME: 5 minutes
YIELD: 1 cup

2 tablespoons Carob Syrup (see page 144)
1 cup milk or soy milk (hot or cold)

1.   Add Carob Syrup to milk.

2.   Stir briskly.

Lemonade

Welcome the summertime with this drink.
It's as cooling as sitting in the shade of a tree.

PREPARATION TIME: 15 minutes
YIELD: 9 half-cup servings

4 tablespoons (¹⁄₄ cup) lemon or lime juice
¹⁄₂ cup honey
4 cups (1 quart) water

1. In a small saucepan, combine lemon juice and honey.

2. Cook and stir mixture on medium heat until it begins to steam. *Do not boil.*

3. Pour mixture into a large pitcher, add water, and stir until ingredients are blended.

4. Serve over ice and garnish with a sprig of mint if desired.

Egg Nog

The perfect liquid dessert

PREPARATION TIME:	20 minutes
CHILLING TIME:	3–4 hours
YIELD:	8–10 half-cup servings

½ tablespoon (½ envelope) unflavored gelatin
¼ cup water
⅓ cup honey
6 large yolks (½ cup)
1 cup (½-pint carton) heavy cream or soy milk
2 cups milk or soy milk
1 teaspoon vanilla
½ teaspoon nutmeg

1. Mix gelatin and water in a cup.

2. Place cup in a bowl of hot water until gelatin is dissolved and mixture is clear. Set aside.

3. In a medium-sized pan, combine honey, egg yolks, and cream. Cook over medium heat, stirring constantly until mixture is hot. *Do not boil.*

4. Add gelatin. Mix and cook for about 2 minutes.

5. Add milk and vanilla. Mix to blend.

6. Pour into 1-quart container through a strainer to remove any bits of undissolved gelatin or egg white.

7. Add nutmeg and stir.

8. Chill for several hours before serving.

Peanut Butter Shake

This surprisingly delicious drink is as satisfying as a full meal.

PREPARATION TIME: 5 minutes
YIELD: 4 half-cup servings

3 tablespoons natural peanut butter, smooth
1 teaspoon vanilla
3 tablespoons honey or 2 tablespoons molasses
2 cups milk or soy milk

1. Combine all ingredients in a blender and mix until smooth.

Bibliography

Dufty, William. *Sugar Blues*. New York: Warner Books, 1975.

Food and Nutrition Encyclopedia, Volume 2. Clovis, California: Pegus Press, 1983.

Johnson, Arnold H. and Martin S. Peterson. *Encyclopedia of Food Technology, Volume 2*. Westport: The Avi Publishing Co., Inc., 1974.

Mindell, Earl. *Vitamin Bible*. New York: Warner Books, 1979.

Remington, D.W., and B. W. Higa. *The Bitter Truth About Artificial Sweeteners*. Provo, Utah: Vitality House International, l987.

Swope, Mary R. *Are You Sick and Tired of Feeling Sick and Tired?* Springdale, Pennsylvania: Whitaker House, 1984.

Winter, Ruth. *A Consumer's Dictionary of Food Additives*. New York: Crown Publishers, Inc., 1978.

Index

Allergies, vii, 1, 4
Angel Food Cake, 22
Apple Cake, 13
Apple Cobbler, 85, 87
Apple Pie, 75
Arrowhead Mills, ii
Aspartame, 1
Asthma, ii

Baked Alaska, 40
Banana Cake, 15
Banana Cream Pudding, 108
Banana Pops, 146
Basic Pie Shell, 65
Basic Yellow Cake, 8
Beverages, 171–184
    Cappuccino Shake, 180
    Carob Drink, 181
    Egg Nog, 183
    Golden Punch, 174
    hints pertaining to, 172
    Holiday Punch, 175
    Iced Cappuccino, 180
    Iced Mocha, 179
    Lemonade, 182
    Milk Shake I, 176
    Milk Shake II, 177
    Mocha Shake, 179
    Peanut Butter Shake, 184
    Rose Punch, 173
    Smoothie, 178

    Wassail, 175
Boston Cream Pie, 17
Bread Pudding, 118
Brownies, 54–55
    double fudge, 55
    peanut butter, 55
Butter, 4
Butter Cream Frosting, 135
Butter Nut Cookies, 60
Butternut Squash Pie, 92
Butterscotch Cream Pudding, 108

Cake Doughnuts, 33
Cakes, 5–41
    angel food, 22
    apple, 13
    baked Alaska, 41
    banana, 15
    basic yellow, 8
    Boston cream, 17
    carob, 10
    carrot, 12
    cheese, 31
    coconut, 9
    crumb, 26
    date, 13
    date crumb, 27
    decoration of, 5
    fruit, 24
    German carob, 11
    gingerbread, 16

hints pertaining to, 6
ice cream sandwich, 38
jelly roll, 35
mini fruit, 25
one-layer carob, 11
orange, 9
pineapple upside-down, 18
pound, 20
pudding, 39
select a pan for, 7
shortcakes, 29
single-layer yellow, 9
spice, 14
streusel, 26
trifle, 28
Yule log, 36
Candy, 123–129, 131–134
carob fudge, 125
divinity, 129
glazed nuts, 126
hints pertaining to, 124
maple fudge, 127
marshmallows, 133
New Orleans pralines, 131
peanut butter fudge, 128
pecan log, 134
pralines, 131
Cappuccino Shake, 180
Carob, 4
Carob Cake, 10
Carob Chiffon Pie, 99
Carob Chip Cookies, 61
Carob Cookies, 47
Carob Cream Frosting, 138
Carob Cream Pudding, 113
Carob Cupcakes, 11
Carob Drink, 181
Carob Fudge, 125
Carob Fudge Frosting, 138
Carob Ice Cream, 154
Carob Mint Cookies, 48
Carob Mint Frosting, 138
Carob Mousse, 163
Carob Soy-Milk Ice Cream, 156
Carob Syrup, 144
Carob Whip, 150
Carrot Cake, 12

Carrot Cupcakes, 13
Cherry Pie, 77
Chess Pie, 93
Cheesecake, 31
Chiffon pie, variations of, 100
Cinnamon Rolls, 71
Cobbler, 85-88
apple, 85, 87
blackberry, 85, 87
blueberry, 85, 87
cherry, 85, 87
fresh fruit, 88
fruit cocktail, 85, 87
peach, 85, 87
pineapple, 85, 87
Cobbler I, 85
Cobbler II, 87
Coconut Cake, 9
Coconut Chess Pie, 94
Coconut Cream Pudding, 108
Cookies, 43–62
bar, 54–55
butter nut, 60
carob, 47
carob chip, 61
carob mint, 48
gingerbread cutouts, 49
graham crackers, 52
hints pertaining to, 44
lemon, 46
macaroons, 56
maple sugar, 51
meringue, 53
mint, 46
oatmeal, 62
orange, 46
peanut butter, 57
spice, 59
thumb-print, 58
vanilla, 45
Cool-Center Crêpes, 167
Cream Cheese Frosting, 130
Cream Pops, 157
Cream Puffs, 73
Crêpes, 167–168
cool-center, 167
dinner, 168

Crumb Cake, 26
Crumb Shell, 70
Crumb Topped Fruit Pies, 78
Cupcakes
    banana, 15
    carob, 11
    carrot, 13
    gingerbread, 17
    spice, 15
    yellow, 9
Custard, 114
Custard Pie, 95

Date Cake, 13
Date Crumb Cake, 27
Date Whip, 148
Digestive problems, 1
Diseases, degenerative, 1
Divinity Candy, 129
Divinity Frosting, 130
Double Fudge Brownies, 55
Doughnuts, 33

Eclairs, 74
Egg Nog, 183

Flan, 115
Flour, processed white, 1
Ford, Frank, iii
Fresh Fruit Cobbler, 88
Fresh Fruit Whip, 149
Frosting
    butter cream, 135
    carob cream, 138
    carob fudge, 126
    carob mint, 138
    cream cheese, 130
    divinity, 130
    fruit cream cheese, 140
    hints pertaining to, 124
    lemon cream, 135
    maple cream, 136
    maple fudge, 127
    non-dairy whipped topping, 136
    orange cream, 136
    peanut butter fudge, 128
    pecan, 139
    whipped cream, 137
Frozen Pops, 157
Fruit Cake, 24
Fruit Cream Cheese Frosting, 140
Fruit Cream Cheese Pie, 103
Fruit Glaze, 141
Fruit Mousse, 159
Fruit salad, 152
Fruit Soy-Milk Ice Cream, 156
Fudge Pops, 158

Gelatin Dessert, 147
German Carob Cake, 11
Gingerbread, 16
    cupcakes, 17
    cutouts, 49
Glazed Nuts, 126
Glazes, 141–144
    carob syrup, 144
    fruit, 141
    lemon sauce, 142
    orange, 143
    pineapple sauce, 143
Golden Punch, 174
Graham Crackers, 52

Hard Sauce, 120
Hints
    beverages, 172
    cakes, 6
    candies, 124
    cookies, 44
    cooling desserts, 146
    frostings, 124
    glazes, 124
    pastries, 64
    pies, 64
    puddings, 106
Holiday Punch, 175
Honey
    reaction to changes in temperature of, 2
    storage of 3,
    sweetness of, 2
Honey Lime Dressing, 152

Ice cream
    cake, 38, 40

carob, 154
carob soy-milk, 156
fruit, 154
fruit soy-milk, 156
vanilla, 153
vanilla soy-milk, 155
waffles and, 169
Ice ring, 172
Iced Cappuccino, 180
Iced Mocha, 179
Indian Pudding, 116
Infection, 1

Jelly Roll, 35
Lactose intolerance, 4
Lemonade, 182
Lemon Cookies, 46
Lemon Cream Frosting, 135
Lemon Cream Pudding, 110
Lemon Meringue Pie, 97
Lemon Pineapple Pudding, 110
Lemon Pudding, 109
Lemon Sauce, 142

Macaroons, 56
Maple Brown Sugar, 132
Maple Cream Frosting, 136
Maple Cream Pudding, 111
Maple Fudge, 127
Maple Fudge Frosting, 127
Maple Mousse, 161
Maple Nut Pudding, 112
Maple Nut Whip, 162
Maple Sugar, 132
Maple Sugar Cookies, 51
Maple syrup
    grades of, 3
    minerals in, 2–4
    nutritional value of, 3
    storage of, 3
Maple Walnut Pie, 90
Marshmallows, 133
Meringue Cookies, 53
Milk Shake I, 176
Milk Shake II, 177
Mincemeatless Pie, 83
Mini Fruit Cakes, 25

Mint Cookies, 46
Mocha Shake, 179
Molasses, 2
    storage of, 2, 3
    unsulphured, 2
Molasses Crumb Pie, 101
Mousse, 159–162, 163–166
    carob, 163
    fruit, 159
    maple, 161
    peanut butter, 165

New Orleans Pralines, 131
Non-Dairy Whipped Topping, 136
Nuts, glazed, 126

Oatmeal Cookies, 62
Oatmeal Pie, 90
Oil, unrefined, 6
One-Layer Carob Cake, 11
Orange Cake, 9
Orange Cookies, 46
Orange Cream Frosting, 136
Orange Sauce, 143

Pancakes, 169
Partially-Baked Pie Shell, 76
Pastries, 63–74, 76
    basic pie shell, 65
    cinnamon rolls, 71
    cream puffs, 73
    crumb shell, 70
    crumb topped fruit pies, 78
    eclairs, 74
    hints pertaining to, 64
    partially-baked pie shell, 76
    quick whole-wheat shell, 69
    whole-wheat pie shell, 67
Peach Pie, 79
Peanut Butter Brownies, 55
Peanut Butter Cookies, 57
Peanut Butter Cream Pudding, 108
Peanut Butter Fudge, 128
Peanut Butter Fudge Frosting, 128
Peanut Butter Mousse, 165
Peanut Butter Shake, 184
Pecan. *See* Nuts, glazed, and Pralines.

Pecan Frosting, 139
Pecan Log, 134
Pecan Pie I, 89
Pecan Pie II, 90
Pies, 63–64, 77–104
  apple, 75
  banana cream. *See* Hints, pies.
  butternut squash, 92
  butterscotch cream. *See* Hints, pies.
  carob chiffon, 99
  carob cream. *See* Hints, pies.
  Cherry, 77
  chess, 93
  cobbler, 85–88
  coconut chess, 94
  coconut cream. *See* Hints, pies.
  crumb topped fruit, 78
  custard, 95
  fruit chiffon. *See* Hints, pies.
  fruit cream cheese, 103
  hints pertaining to, 64
  lemon. *See* Hints, pies.
  lemon cream. *See* Hints, pies.
  lemon meringue, 97
  lemon pineapple pie. *See* Hints, pies.
  maple chiffon. *See* Hints, pies.
  maple cream. *See* Hints, pies.
  maple nut pie. *See* Hints, pies.
  maple walnut, 90
  mincemeatless, 83
  molasses crumb, 101
  oatmeal, 90
  peach, 79
  peanut butter chiffon. *See* Hints, pies.
  peanut butter cream. *See* Hints, pies.
  pecan, 89–90
  pineapple, 81
  pumpkin, 91
  shoo-fly, 101
  sweet potato, 92
  vanilla cream. *See* Hints, pies.
Pineapple Cobbler, 85, 87
Pineapple Pie, 81
Pineapple Sauce, 143
Pineapple Upside-Down Cake, 18
Plum Pudding, 120
Pops, frozen, 146, 157–158

  banana, 146
  cream, 157
  fudge, 158
  mousse, 146
  pudding, 158
Pound Cake, 20
Pralines, 131
Prune Whip, 149
Pudding Cake, 39
Pudding Pops, 158
Puddings, 105–121
  banana cream, 108
  bread, 118
  butterscotch cream, 108
  carob cream, 113
  coconut cream, 108
  custard, 114
  flan, 115
  hints pertaining to, 106
  Indian, 116
  lemon, 109
  lemon cream, 110
  lemon pineapple, 110
  maple cream, 111
  maple nut, 112
  peanut butter cream, 108
  plum, 120
  rice, 119
  vanilla cream, 107
Pumpkin Pie, 91
Punch, 173–175
  golden, 174
  holiday, 175
  rose, 173
  wassail, 175

Quick Whole-Wheat Pie Shell, 69

Rice Pudding, 119
Rose Punch, 173

Salt
  sea, 3,4
  table, 3, 4
Sauces
  hard, 120
  lemon, 142

    orange, 143
    pineapple, 143
Shakes, 176–180, 184
    cappuccino, 180
    milk, 176–177
    mocha, 179
    peanut butter, 184
    smoothie, 178
Shoo-Fly Pie. *See* Molasses Crumb Pie.
Shortcake, large, 30
Shortckes, individual, 29
Shortening, Smither, 66
Single-Layer Cake, 9
Smither Shortening, 66
Smoothie, 178
Soy margarine, 4
Soy milk, 4
Spice Cake, 14
Spice Cookies, 59
Spice Cupcakes, 15
Streusel, 26
Sugar
    brown, 1
    processed white, 1
Sweet Potato Pie, 92
Sweeteners
    artificial, 1
    natural, 2–3

Trifle, 28
Thumb-Print Cookies, 58

Vanilla Cookies, 45
Vanilla Cream Pudding, 107
Vanilla Ice Cream, 153
Vanilla Soy-Milk Ice Cream, 155

Waffles and Ice Cream, 169
Wassail, 175
Whipped Cream Frosting, 137
Whipped Topping, non-dairy, 136
Whips, 148–151, 162
    carob, 150
    coffee, 151
    date, 148
    fresh fruit, 149
    maple nut, 162
    prune, 149
Whole-Wheat Pie Shell, 67

Yellow cake
    basic, 8
    cupcakes, 9
    single-layer, 9
Yule Log, 36